Workbook for

Tonal Harmony

Workbook for
Tonal Harmony

with an Introduction to Post-Tonal Music

Eighth Edition

Stefan Kostka
The University of Texas at Austin

Dorothy Payne
The University of South Carolina

Byron Almén
The University of Texas at Austin

McGraw Hill Education

WORKBOOK FOR TONAL HARMONY WITH AN INTRODUCTION TO POST-TONAL MUSIC, EIGHTH EDITION

Published by McGraw-Hill Education, 2 Penn Plaza, New York, NY 10121. Copyright © 2018 by McGraw-Hill Education. All rights reserved. Printed in the United States of America. Previous editions © 2013, 2009, and 2004. No part of this publication may be reproduced or distributed in any form or by any means, or stored in a database or retrieval system, without the prior written consent of McGraw-Hill Education, including, but not limited to, in any network or other electronic storage or transmission, or broadcast for distance learning.

Some ancillaries, including electronic and print components, may not be available to customers outside the United States.

This book is printed on acid-free paper.

11 12 LON 23

ISBN   978-1-259-68676-4
MHID   1-259-68676-0

Cover Image: © *Archiwiz/Getty Images*

www.mhhe.com

Contents

PART I
Fundamentals 1

CHAPTER 1
Elements of Pitch   1

CHAPTER 2
Elements of Rhythm   11

CHAPTER 3
Introduction to Triads
and Seventh Chords   19

CHAPTER 4
Diatonic Chords in Major
and Minor Keys   31

PART II
Diatonic Triads   35

CHAPTER 5
Principles of Voice Leading   35

CHAPTER 6
Root-Position Part Writing   41

CHAPTER 7
Harmonic Progression and
the Sequence   55

CHAPTER 8
Triads in First Inversion   61

CHAPTER 9
Triads in Second Inversion   71

CHAPTER 10
Cadences, Phrases, Periods,
and Sentences   79

CHAPTER 11
Two-Part Tonal Counterpoint   87

CHAPTER 12
Nonchord Tones 1   91

CHAPTER 13
Nonchord Tones 2   99

PART III
Diatonic Seventh Chords   105

CHAPTER 14
The V^7 Chord   105

CHAPTER 15
Other Diatonic Seventh
Chords   123

PART IV
Chromaticism 1   133

CHAPTER 16
Secondary Functions 1   133

CHAPTER 17
Secondary Functions 2   147

CHAPTER 18
Modulations Using Diatonic
Common Chords   161

CHAPTER 19
Some Other Modulatory
Techniques   177

CHAPTER 20
Larger Forms   185

PART V
Chromaticism 2   203

CHAPTER 21
Mode Mixture and
the Neapolitan   203

CHAPTER 22
Augmented Sixth Chords   217

CHAPTER 23
Enharmonic Spellings and
Enharmonic Modulations   231

CHAPTER 24
Further Elements of the Harmonic
Vocabulary   243

CHAPTER 25
Tonal Harmony in the Late
Nineteenth Century   253

PART VI
An Introduction to Twentieth-Century Music   269

CHAPTER 26
Materials and Techniques   269

CHAPTER 27
Post-Tonal Theory   297

CHAPTER 28
New Directions   319

 This icon denotes a listening example.

Chapter 1

ELEMENTS OF PITCH

EXERCISE 1-1

A. Name the pitches in the blanks provided, using the correct octave register designations.

B. Notate the indicated pitches on the staff in the correct octave.

A4   F5   D6   C4   F2   C3   E4   B3   G4   E3   D4   A3

G2   C5   F3   B4   E2   A5   D3   G4   B♭   D5   F4   A3   C2   E6

EXERCISE 1-2

A. Notate the specified scales using accidentals, *not* key signatures. Show the placement of whole and half steps, as in the example.

B. Identify these major key signatures.

_C_ major	_D_ major	_F#_ major	_Db_ major	_Bb_ major	_B_ major	_A_ major	_Cb_ major
ex.	**1**	**2**	**3**	**4**	**5**	**6**	**7**

C. Notate the specified key signatures.

Ab major   E major   F major   C major

Gb major   G major   Eb major   C# major

D. Fill in the blanks.

Key signature	*Name of key*		*Key signature*	*Name of key*
1. _____	D♭ major		**8.** seven flats	____ major
2. _____	G major		**9.** _____	F major
3. five sharps	____ major		**10.** _____	E major
4. _____	E♭ major		**11.** two sharps	____ major
5. two flats	____ major		**12.** three flats	____ major
6. three sharps	____ major		**13.** _____	G♭ major
7. _____	C♯ major		**14.** six sharps	____ major

E. Fill in the blanks, using the example as a model.

	Major Key	*Key Signature*	*Scale Degree*	*Is This Note*
Ex.	C	0♯/0♭	$\hat{5}$	G
1.	E		$\hat{3}$	
2.		2♯		C♯
3.			$\hat{4}$	E♭
4.	G♭			E♭
5.		3♯	$\hat{2}$	
6.		6♯		C♯

EXERCISE 1-3

A. Notate the specified scales using accidentals, not key signatures. The melodic minor should be written both ascending and descending.

c (natural)　　　　　　　　　　　　e (harmonic)

b (natural)　　　　　　　　　　　　a♭ (harmonic)

g (melodic)

a♯ (natural)　　　　　　　　　　　d (harmonic)

d♯ (melodic)

B. Identify the type of each scale as major, natural minor, harmonic minor, or melodic minor. Any melodic minor scales will be shown in the ascending version only.

1. _B♯ Melodic_　　　　　　　2. _B♭ Harmonic_

3. _F♯ Harmonic_　　　　　　　4. _D♭ Harmonic_

5. _F Melodic_　　　　　　　6. _C♯ Natural_

C. Identify these minor key signatures.

_a_ minor	_D_ minor	_C_ minor	_B_ minor	_Bb_ minor	_G#_ minor	_F#_ minor	_A#_ minor
ex.	**1**	**2**	**3**	**4**	**5**	**6**	**7**

D. Notate the specified minor key signatures.

eb minor   c# minor   g minor   a minor

e minor   ab minor   d# minor   f minor

E. Fill in the blanks.

Key signature	Name of key		Key signature	Name of key
1. three sharps	f# minor	**8.** _2 flats_	g minor
2. _6 flats_	eb minor	**9.** two sharps	_B_ minor
3. _four sharps_	c# minor	**10.** seven flats	_Ab_ minor
4. five flats	_Bb_ minor	**11.** _1 sharp_	e minor
5. _0_	a minor	**12.** one flat	_D_ minor
6. four flats	_F_ minor	**13.** _3 flats_	c minor
7. seven sharps	_A#_ minor	**14.** _5 sharps_	g# minor

EXERCISE 1-4

A. Provide the numerical names of the intervals by using the numbers 1 through 8.

$$\underline{\quad} \quad \underline{\quad} \quad \underline{\quad} \quad \underline{\quad} \quad \underline{\quad} \quad \underline{\quad} \quad \underline{\quad} \quad \underline{\quad} \quad \underline{\quad} \quad \underline{\quad} \quad \underline{\quad} \quad \underline{\quad} \quad \underline{\quad} \quad \underline{\quad} \quad \underline{\quad}$$

1 **2** **3** **4** **5** **6** **7** **8** **9** **10** **11** **12** **13** **14** **15**

EXERCISE 1-5

A. All the following intervals are unisons, 4ths, 5ths, or octaves. Put a "P" in the space provided *only* if the interval is a perfect interval.

4	5	8	4	1	5	4	5	4	1
1	**2**	**3**	**4**	**5**	**6**	**7**	**8**	**9**	**10**

5	5	8	5	4	1	4	8	5	4
11	**12**	**13**	**14**	**15**	**16**	**17**	**18**	**19**	**20**

B. All the following intervals are 2nds, 3rds, 6ths, or 7ths. Put an "M" or an "m" in each space, as appropriate.

6	3	2	7	3	7	6	2	3	7
1	**2**	**3**	**4**	**5**	**6**	**7**	**8**	**9**	**10**

6	3	3	7	6	3	2	7	6	7
11	**12**	**13**	**14**	**15**	**16**	**17**	**18**	**19**	**20**

C. Notate the specified intervals above the given notes.

EXERCISE 1-6

A. Most of the intervals that follow are either augmented or diminished. Name each interval.

| 1 | 2 | 3 | 4 | 5 | 6 | 7 | 8 | 9 | 10 |

| 11 | 12 | 13 | 14 | 15 | 16 | 17 | 18 | 19 | 20 |

B. Label what each interval becomes when it is inverted.

1. m3 becomes _____

2. ⁺5 becomes _____

3. M6 becomes _____

4. °7 becomes _____

5. M2 becomes _____

6. ⁺4 becomes _____

7. P5 becomes _____

8. m7 becomes _____

C. Notate the specified interval *below* the given note. (You might find it helpful to invert the interval first in some cases.)

| M7 | P4 | m6 | +2 | m7 | M3 | +6 | °5 | +4 | M6 |
| 1 | 2 | 3 | 4 | 5 | 6 | 7 | 8 | 9 | 10 |

| m2 | M3 | +6 | M2 | °5 | m3 | °7 | P4 | +2 | +4 |
| 11 | 12 | 13 | 14 | 15 | 16 | 17 | 18 | 19 | 20 |

m7	P5	m3	m2	P4	M7	m2	°5	M2	+6
21	22	23	24	25	26	27	28	29	30

m6	P4	M3	P5	+2	m3	P5	°7	M2	M6
31	32	33	34	35	36	37	38	39	40

D. Label each interval in this melody (from Wagner's *Götterdämmerung*). Interval 10 is from the F4 to the C5. Remember that an accidental remains in effect until the end of the measure, unless it is canceled.

E. Beneath each harmonic interval that follows, indicate whether it is consonant ("c"), dissonant ("d"), or dissonant only if the bass has the bottom note of the interval ("d bass").

	1. m3	2. M7	3. +6	4. P5	5. M6
c	___	___	___	___	___
d	___	___	___	___	___
d bass	___	___	___	___	___

	6. °5	7. P4	8. P8	9. m2	10. M3
c	___	___	___	___	___
d	___	___	___	___	___
d bass	___	___	___	___	___

Chapter 2

ELEMENTS OF RHYTHM

EXERCISE 2-1

A. Show how many notes or rests of the shorter duration would be required to equal the longer duration.

ex. 𝅗𝅥 × __2__ = 𝅝

1. ♩ × _____ = 𝅗𝅥

2. ♪ × _____ = 𝅗𝅥

3. 𝅘𝅥𝅯 × _____ = ♩ ♪

4. 𝄿 × _____ = 𝄾·

5. 𝄼 × _____ = 𝄾

6. 𝄻 × _____ = 𝅝

7. ♩ × _____ = 𝄽

8. 𝅘𝅥𝅯 × _____ = ♪·

9. 𝅘𝅥𝅰 × _____ = ♩

10. 𝅗𝅥· × _____ = 𝅗𝅥·

11. 𝅘𝅥𝅯 × _____ = ♩·

12. 𝄿 × _____ = 𝄿

13. 𝄾· × _____ = 𝄻·

14. 𝄿 × _____ = 𝄼·

15. ♪ × _____ = 𝅗𝅥··

16. ♪ × _____ = 𝅝

B. Sing aloud each of the following songs. Then identify the meter type of each, using the terms *duple*, *triple*, and *quadruple*.

1. "Auld Lang Syne" _____

2. "Star-Spangled Banner" _____

3. "Pop Goes the Weasel" _____

4. "America" ("My Country, 'Tis of Thee") _____

5. "Swing Low, Sweet Chariot" _____

C. Scale review. Fill in the blanks, using the melodic minor for all minor-key examples.

ex. $\hat{6}$ is F♯ in __A__ (M)

1. ↓$\hat{7}$ is C in _____ (m)

2. $\hat{4}$ is _____ in c♯

3. _____ is A in F

4. $\hat{5}$ is C♯ in _____ (m)

5. $\hat{2}$ is _____ in E

6. $\hat{7}$ is A in _____ (M)

7. ↓$\hat{6}$ is _____ in c

8. _____ is C♯ in b

9. $\hat{6}$ is C in _____ (M)

10. _____ is F♯ in g

11. $\hat{4}$ is G in _____ (M)

12. $\hat{5}$ is _____ in G

13. _____ is A♭ in f

14. ↑$\hat{6}$ is C♯ in _____ (m)

EXERCISE 2-2

A. Fill in the blanks.

	Beat and Meter Type	Beat Note	Division of the Beat	Time Signature
1.				𝄵
2.	Simple triple	𝅗𝅥		
3.	Simple duple		♫	
4.		♪		2
5.	Simple quadruple		♫	

B. Renotate the excerpts from textbook Example 2-1 using the specified time signatures. (p. 28)

"Jingle Bells"

"America the Beautiful"

"Home on the Range"

EXERCISE 2-3

A. Fill in the blanks.

	Beat and Meter Type	Beat Note	Division of the Beat	Time Signature
1.	Compound triple	♩.		
2.				6 16
3.			♪♪♪ (beamed)	12
4.	Compound duple		♪ ♪ ♪	
5.		♪.		9

B. Renotate the excerpts from textbook Example 2-2 using the specified time signatures. (p. 30)

"Take Me Out to the Ball Game"

"Down in the Valley"

"Pop Goes the Weasel"

EXERCISE 2-4

A. Fill in the blanks.

	Beat and Meter Type	Beat Note	Division of the Beat	Time Signature
1.	Compound quadruple			12/8
2.	Simple triple			3/8
3.	Simple Quadruple			4/2
4.	compound tripple			6/16
5.	Simple double			¢
6.	compound tripple			9/4

B. Each measure below is incomplete. Add one or more rests to the end of each to complete the measure.

C. Provide the best time signature for each exercise. In some cases, more than one correct answer might be possible.

1. ___

7. ___

2. ___

8. ___

3. ___

9. ___

4. ___

10. ___

5. ___

11. ___

6. ___

12. ___

D. Each of the following fragments is notated so that the placement of the beats is obscured in some fashion. Without changing the way the music will sound, rewrite each one to clarify the beat placement. This may involve breaking some of the long notes into tied shorter notes or rebeaming groups of notes.

1. $\frac{4}{4}$ $\frac{4}{4}$ _____

2. $\frac{3}{2}$ $\frac{3}{2}$ _____

3. $\frac{9}{8}$ $\frac{9}{8}$ _____

4. $\frac{2}{4}$ $\frac{2}{4}$ _____

5. $\frac{12}{16}$ $\frac{12}{16}$ _____

6. $\frac{6}{2}$ $\frac{6}{2}$ _____

E. Add stems as required.

1. Each duration is a half note.

2. Each duration is a sixteenth note. Beam them in groups of four.

F. Scale review. Fill in the key, scale degree, or note, whichever is missing. Assume the melodic minor form for all minor keys.

G. Interval review. Notate the specified interval above the given note.

H. Interval review. Notate the specified interval below the given note.

Chapter 3

INTRODUCTION TO TRIADS AND SEVENTH CHORDS

EXERCISE 3-1

A. Spell the triad, given the root and the type. Major triads are indicated by an uppercase letter (G), minor by an uppercase letter followed by the letter "m" (Gm), augmented by a "+" (G+), and diminished by a "°" (G°).

1. Gm   _G bb D_
2. E♭   _bE G bb_
3. D°   _D F♭ A_
4. A°   _A C ♭e_
5. Fm   _F ♭a C_
6. D♭   _b♭ F ♭A_
7. C+   _C E #G_
8. A#°   _#A #C E_
9. E   _E #G B_
10. F#m   _#F A #C_
11. B+   _B#D XF_
12. E♭m   _E♭ b b G_

B. Notate the triad, given the root and the type.

19

C. Fill in the blanks.

	ex.	1	2	3	4	5	6	7	8	9	10
5th:	G♯	A♭	___	F♯	___	___	___	___	___	B	___
3rd:	E	___	___	___	___	E♭	___	___	B♭	___	A
Root:	C♯	___	D	___	A♭	___	G♯	E♭	___	___	___
Type:	m	M	+	m	m	°	m	M	+	m	°

D. Given the chord quality and one member of the triad, notate the remainder of the triad.

EXERCISE 3-2

A. Identify the type of seventh chord, using the abbreviations given in Example 3-3. (p. 40)

Mm7 ____ ____ ____ ____ ____ ____ ____

____ ____ ____ ____ ____ ____ ____ ____

B. Notate the seventh chord, given the root and type.

M7   Mm7   M7   ø7   Mm7   M7   °7   Mm7

ø7   m7   ø7   m7   °7   m7   Mm7   °7

C. Given the seventh-chord quality and one member of the chord, notate the rest of the chord.

5th   7th   3rd   5th   5th   3rd   7th   root
m7   M7   m7   ø7   m7   Mm7   ø7   M7

7th   root   3rd   3rd   5th   root   7th   5th
°7   Mm7   M7   m7   °7   m7   ø7   °7

EXERCISE 3-3

A. Identify the root and type of each chord and show the correct bass-position symbol (Bps).

Root   ___ ___ ___ ___   ___ ___ ___ ___

Type   ___ ___ ___ ___   ___ ___ ___ ___

Bps   ___ ___ ___ ___   ___ ___ ___ ___

Root   ___ ___ ___ ___ ___ ___ ___ ___

Type   ___ ___ ___ ___ ___ ___ ___ ___

Bps   ___ ___ ___ ___ ___ ___ ___ ___

B. Fill in the blanks below each figured bass with the lead-sheet symbol of the chord that would be played at the corresponding point in the excerpt. Use slash-chord notation, as in C/E, for inverted chords. The figures 5 and $\frac{5}{3}$ both mean to use a root position triad.

1. Bach, "Gott lebet noch" (adapted)

___ ___ ___ ___ ___ ___ ___ ___ ___ ___ ___ ___ ___
 1   2   3   4   5   6   7   8   9 10 11 12 13

2. Bach, "Dich bet' ich an, mein höchster Gott"

(The first C♯3 in the bass is not to be harmonized.)

___ ___ ___ ___ ___ ___ ___ ___ ___ ___ ___ ___ ___ ___ ___ ___
 1   2   3   4   5   6   7   8   9 10 11 12 13 14 15 16

3. Corelli, Sonata V, op. 2, Sarabande

C. Notate using half notes on the bottom staff the chords indicated by the lead-sheet
symbols. Notate all chords in root position.

 Terry, "Serenade to a Bus Seat"

This icon is used throughout this workbook to indicate the availability of a corresponding
audio excerpt, which is available exclusively in McGraw-Hill Connect.

EXERCISE 3-4

A. Label each chord with an appropriate lead-sheet symbol in the space above the chord.
    Use slash-chord notation for inverted chords. All the notes in each exercise belong to
    the same chord.

B. Provide the root, type, and bass-position symbol (Bps) for each chord in the following excerpts. Each chord is numbered. Put your analysis of the chords in the blanks below each excerpt.

1. Bach, "Wer weiss, wie nahe mir mein Ende"

Root

Type

Bps
   1   2   3   4   5   6   7   8   9 10 11 12 13 14 15 16 17

Root

Type

Bps
 18 19 20 21 22 23 24 25 26 27 28 29 30 31 32 33 34

2. Schumann, "Ich will meine Seele tauchen," op. 48, no. 5

Leise

Ich will   mei - ne   See - le   tau - chen   in   den

Root ____   ____   ____   ____

Type ____   ____   ____   ____

Bps

1   **2**   **3**   **4**

Kelch   der   Li -   lie   hin - ein,   die

Root ____   ____   ____   ____

Type ____   ____   ____   ____

Bps

5   **6**   **7**   **8**

Root ____ ____ ____ ____

Type ____ ____ ____ ____

Bps ____ ____ ____ ____
     9   **10**   **11**   **12**

Root ____ ____ ____ ____ ____ ____ ____

Type ____ ____ ____ ____ ____ ____ ____

Bps ____ ____ ____ ____ ____ ____ ____
    13 **14** **15** **16** **17** **18** **19**

3. Gottschalk, "Jerusalem"

Root
Type
Bps

1   **2**   **3**   **4**

Root
Type
Bps

5   **6**   **7**   **8**   **9**

C. Time signature review. Fill in the blanks.

	Beat and Meter Type	Beat Note	Division of the Beat	Time Signature
1.	Simple triple		♬	
2.			♬♪	9
3.		𝅗𝅥.		6
4.				4 16

Chapter 4

DIATONIC CHORDS IN MAJOR AND MINOR KEYS

EXERCISE 4-1

A. Given the key and the triad, supply the roman numeral *below* the staff. Be sure your roman numeral is of the correct type (correct case and so on), and include bass-position symbols (6 or $^6_4$) where needed. Finally, provide an appropriate lead-sheet symbol *above* the staff, using slash-chord notation where appropriate.

B. In the following exercise you are given the name of a key and a scale degree number (in parentheses). *Without using key signatures*, notate the triad on that scale degree, and provide the roman numeral. In minor keys, be sure to use the triad types circled in Example 4-7. (p. 57)

31

C. Analysis. Write roman numerals in the spaces provided, making sure each roman numeral is of the correct type and includes a bass-position symbol if necessary.

 1. Handel, "Wenn mein Stündlein vorhanden ist"

Bb: _____ _____ _____ _____ _____ _____ _____ _____
  1   2   3   4   5   6   7   8

 2. Handel, "Wenn mein Stündlein vorhanden ist"

Bb: _____ _____ _____ _____ _____ _____ _____ _I_
  1   2   3   4   5   6   7   8

D. Fill in the blanks, using the example as a model.

	Key	This Chord	Has This Bass Note
ex.	C	I^6	E
1.	a	V^6	
2.		IV^6	C
3.	c#	ii^{o6}	
4.	B	$^6_4$	C#
5.		i$^{o6}_4$	D
6.	F	vii^{o6}	

EXERCISE 4-2

A. Given the key and the seventh chord, supply the roman numeral *below* the staff. Be sure your roman numeral is of the correct type, and include bass-position symbols where needed. Finally, provide an appropriate lead-sheet symbol *above* the staff.

ex. G#°7   1 ___   2 ___   3 ___   4 ___   5 ___   6 ___   7 ___

a: *vii*°7   G: ___   c#: ___   f: ___   B♭: ___   e: ___   A♭: ___   g: ___

8 ___   9 ___   10 ___   11 ___   12 ___   13 ___   14 ___   15 ___

d: ___   E: ___   F: ___   A: ___   E♭: ___   b: ___   c: ___   D: ___

B. In the following exercises, you are given the name of a key and a scale degree number (in parentheses). *Without using key signatures,* notate the seventh chord on that scale degree in root position, and provide the roman numeral. In minor keys, be sure to use the chord types shown in Example 4-9. (p. 62)

ex.   1   2   3   4   5   6   7

G: *iii*7   B♭: ___   F: ___   b: ___   f#: ___   A: ___   g: ___   D: ___
(3̂)   (4̂)   (1̂)   (3̂)   (2̂)   (7̂)   (7̂)   (6̂)

8   9   10   11   12   13   14   15

c: ___   E: ___   G: ___   E♭: ___   c#: ___   f: ___   e: ___   A♭: ___
(1̂)   (4̂)   (2̂)   (3̂)   (5̂)   (5̂)   (2̂)   (6̂)

C. Analysis. Put roman numerals in the spaces provided, making sure each roman numeral is of the correct type and includes a bass-position symbol, if needed. For the purposes of this exercise, ignore the G5 in m. 3.

 1. Hummel, German Dance, op. 25, no. 2, Trio 2

Be sure to include tied notes (like the E-flats in mm. 2–3) in your analyses of both measures in which they are found.

 2. Brahms, "Minnelied," op. 44, no. 1

Part II

Diatonic Triads

Chapter 5

PRINCIPLES OF VOICE LEADING

EXERCISE 5-1

A. Criticize each melody in terms of the rules for simple melodies discussed in The Melodic Line section on pages 66–69.

B. Compose simple melodies that will conform to these progressions.

2

d: i   V   VI   iv   i   V   i   iv   V   i

3

G: I   iii   IV   I   V   I   IV   V   I

EXERCISE 5-2

A. Analyze the following excerpt using roman numerals and bass-position symbols. Then, show beneath each roman numeral the structure of the chord by writing "C" or "O" for close or open structure. The notes in parentheses are not part of the chord and should be ignored for the purpose of harmonic analysis.

 Schumann, "Roundelay," op. 68, no. 22

B. Review the two conventions concerning spacing in Voicing a Single Triad on pages 70–72. Then point out in the following example any places where those conventions are not followed.

C. Fill in the circled missing inner voice(s) to complete each root-position triad, being
    sure that each note of the triad is represented. Follow the spacing conventions, and stay
    within the range of each vocal part.

D. In the following examples, you are given the soprano note for each chord. Supply the
    alto, tenor, and bass notes to complete the specified triad in close or open position, as
    indicated. Be sure to double the root of each chord and follow the spacing conventions.

EXERCISE 5-3

A. First, put lead-sheet symbols in the blanks above this example. Then analyze the motion between each of the pairs of voices, and fill in the blanks using this system:

st = static   o = oblique   c = contrary   s = similar   p = parallel

1. Bass/Soprano   ____ ____ ____

2. Bass/Alto   ____ ____ ____

3. Bass/Tenor   ____ ____ ____

4. Tenor/Soprano   ____ ____ ____

5. Tenor/Alto   ____ ____ ____

6. Alto/Soprano   ____ ____ ____

B. Label the chords in the following excerpt with roman numerals. Then label *any* parallel motion that you find between any two voices.

Bach, "Ermuntre dich, mein schwacher Geist"

C. Find and label the following errors in this passage:

  1. Parallel 8ves

  2. Parallel 5ths

  3. Direct 5th

  4. Contrary 5ths

  5. Spacing error (review pp. 70–72)

D. Find and label the following errors in this passage:

  1. Parallel 8ves

  2. Parallel 5ths

  3. Direct 8ve

  4. Spacing error

Chapter 6

ROOT-POSITION PART WRITING

EXERCISE 6-1. *Using repeated triads*

A. Fill in the inner voice or voices in the second chord of each exercise. The key is F major throughout. Double the roots of the triads in the four-voice examples.

1 four parts

2 three parts

EXERCISE 6-2. *Using roots a 4th (5th) apart*

A. Add alto and tenor parts to each of the following exercises. Each progression involves roots a P4 (P5) apart. Use one of the three methods outlined in Root Position Part Writing with Roots a 4th (5th) Apart on pages 83–84 in each case, and state which you have used.

c: V   i   G: ii   V   I   V   Eb: iii   vi   ii   V   I

b: i   iv   i   V   i   F: vi   ii   V   I   IV   I   V   I

a: V   i   iv   i   D: iii   vi   ii   V   I   V   I

B. Add an alto part to each exercise. Be careful to observe conventions concerning spacing, parallels, and doubling. Each triad should include at least a root and a 3rd.

EXERCISE 6-3. *Using roots a 4th (5th) and 3rd (6th) apart*

A. Add alto and tenor parts to each exercise that follows. Use the smoothest voice leading
    in each case. For roots a 4th (5th) apart, state which method you have used.

F: I   vi   IV   ii   g: i   V   i   VI   iv   i   D: I   vi   ii   V   I

Eb: I   iii   vi   ii   V   I   e: i   VI   iv   i   V   i

B. Add an alto part to each exercise that follows. Be careful to observe the conventions
    concerning parallels, spacing, and doubling.

Eb: IV   ii   V   I   b: i   III   VI   iv   i   G: I   V   I   IV   ii   V   I

F: I   IV   ii   V   I   d: i   iv   i   VI   iv   i   V   i

EXERCISE 6-4. *Using all root relationships*

A. Complete each progression. Make two versions of each: one for three parts (adding an alto) and one for four parts (adding alto and tenor). In the four-part versions, state which method you have used for any progression by 4th or 5th.

1 three parts   four parts

g: i   III   VI   i   III   VI

2

D: ii   V   vi   ii   V   vi

3

a: iv   V   VI   iv   V   VI

4

B♭:   V   I   vi   V   I   vi

5

G: I   vi   V   I   vi   V

6

F: vi   ii   V   vi   ii   V

B.   Fill in alto and tenor parts in these exercises.

5

d:　　　i　　　IV　　V　　i　　III　　iv　　V　　i　　VI　　iv　　V　　i

$\left(\begin{smallmatrix}not\\iv\end{smallmatrix}\right)$

C. Name the keys and analyze the chords specified by these figured basses. Then compose a good melody line for each. Finally, fill in alto and tenor parts to make a four-part texture.

1

2

D. Write the following short progressions in root position for combinations of three and four parts.

1 three parts

Eb: ii   V   I   c#:   i   VI   iv   A: IV   V   vi

2 four parts

Eb: ii   V   I   c#:   i   VI   iv   A: IV   V   vi

3 three parts

F: I   iii   IV   D: vi   ii   V   g: VI   iv   V

4 four parts

F: I   iii   IV   D: vi   ii   V   g: VI   iv   V

EXERCISE 6-5

A. Notate the following chords for the specified instruments. Each chord is written at concert pitch, so transpose as needed for the performers. You do not need to use key signatures, but use the correct clef for each instrument. Note that the instruments are listed in score order, the order used in Appendix A, which is not always the same as order by pitch.

Fl.	Ob.	Clar. in B♭	Bsn.	A. Sax

T. Sax.	Hn. in F	Tpt. in B♭	Trb.	Hn. in F

Vla.	Vl.	Vc.	D.B.	Tuba

B. Set the following progression for combinations of three and four parts. If possible, score for instruments in your class. Use root position only.

1 three parts (reduced score)

d: i   iv   V   VI   iv   V   i

(full score)

2 four parts (reduced score)

d: i   iv   V   VI   iv   V   i

(full score)

C. Write a version of the following excerpt on a grand staff by transposing the parts to concert pitch. Play your version on the piano and analyze the harmonies if you can.

Chapter 7

HARMONIC PROGRESSION AND THE SEQUENCE

EXERCISE 7-1

A. Complete each harmonic fragment to conform with the major-mode diagram presented on page 105. The chord in the blank should be different from those on either side of it.

1. IV   _?_   I   (___ or ___)   **4.** iii   _?_   V   (___)

2. vi   _?_   I   (___)   **5.** vii°   _?_   vi   (___)

3. I   _?_   ii   (___ or ___)   **6.** vi   _?_   ii   (___)

B. Bracket any portions of these progressions that do not conform to the chord diagrams on page 105.

1. i   vii°   i   iv   VI   V   i

2. I   vi   ii   IV   I   V   I

3. I   iii   IV   vii°   I   IV   V   I

4. i   III   iv   i   iv   V   vii°   i

C. Analysis. Label all chords with roman numerals and bass-position symbols. Bracket any successions of roman numerals that do not agree with the complete major and minor chord diagrams. In addition, provide lead-sheet symbols above the top staff.

 1. Bach, "Du Friedensfürst, Herr Jesu Christ"

2. Vivaldi, Cello Sonata in G Minor, Prelude. Unfigured bass realization by S. Kostka.

Nonchord tones in the solo part have not been put in parentheses, but the harmonic analysis can be done by concentrating on the accompaniment. The key is g minor, despite what appears to be an incorrect key signature. Key signatures had not yet become standardized when this work was composed.

D. Analyze the chords specified by these figured basses and add inner voices to make a four-part texture. Bracket all circle-of-fifths progressions, even those that contain only two chords. Before beginning, review the part writing for deceptive progressions on pages 88–89.

1

2

3

E. Analyze this figured bass, then add a good soprano line and inner voices. Bracket all circle-of-fifths progressions.

F. Add an alto part (only) to mm. 1–2. Then compose a good soprano line for mm. 3–4 and fill in an alto part.

F: I   V   I   vi   IV   V   I   vi   ii   V   I   V   I

G. Following are two unfigured bass lines. Using triads in root position and first inversion *only*, show a good harmonization of each one by placing roman numerals beneath the bass line. Be sure to refer to the diagrams on page 105 while you work on your harmonizations.

1

2

Name_____ Class_____ Date_____

H. Harmonize the following melodies by using root-position major or minor (not diminished) triads in an acceptable progression. Try to give the bass a good contour while avoiding parallel and direct 5ths and 8ves with the melody. Be sure to include analysis. Finally, add one or two inner parts to make a version for SAB three-part chorus or SATB four-part chorus, as indicated.

1 SATB

G:

2 SAB

D:
or b:

3 SATB

E♭:

4 SATB

E:

I. Compose a *simple* melody, then follow the instructions for Part H. You might need to revise the melody as you work on the harmonization.

J. Review: Label the chords with roman numerals and bass-position symbols (where needed).

c: _iv⁶_   f: ____   B♭: ____   G: ____   d: ____   b: ____   E: ____   A♭: ____

f♯: ____   g: ____   E♭: ____   D: ____   e: ____   c♯: ____   F: ____   A: ____

Chapter 8

TRIADS IN FIRST INVERSION

EXERCISE 8-1

A. Analysis.

1. a. Bracket the longest series of parallel sixth chords (triads in first inversion) that you can find in this excerpt. Do not attempt a roman numeral analysis.

b. Does the voice leading in the sixth-chord passage resemble more closely Example 8-9 (p. 119) or Example 8-10 (p. 120)?

   Beethoven, Piano Sonata op. 2, no. 1, III

2. a. Label all chords with roman numerals.

b. Then classify the doubling in each inverted triad according to the methods shown in Example 8-11 (p. 121).

 Bach, "Was frag' ich nach der Welt"

3. a. Provide lead-sheet symbols (including slash chords) above the excerpt and roman numerals beneath it.

b. Bracket the circle-of-fifths progression (review pp. 96–98).

 Handel, Passacaglia

B. The following excerpt is from Mozart's String Quartet, K. 428. Supply the missing tenor line (viola in the original).

C. Supply alto and tenor lines for the following passages.

D. Supply alto lines for the following passages.

g: i⁶   iv⁶   ii°⁶   V   A: V   I⁶   V⁶   I   f: i   vii°⁶   i⁶   ii°⁶   V

d: i   i⁶   iv   i⁶   b: i   IV   vii°⁶   i   E♭:   I   IV⁶   V⁶   I

E. Analyze the harmonies implied by the following soprano/bass lines and add one or two inner parts, as specified by your instructor.

F:

e:

F. The following passage is reduced from Beethoven's Sonata op. 10, no. 3, III. Analyze the implied harmonies (more than one good solution is possible), and add an alto line (only). Use only triads in root position and first inversion.

G. Continue your solution to Part D with a second eight-measure segment. The second part should be similar to the first, but if it starts exactly like it, objectionable parallels will result. Maintain the three-part texture.

H. Review the figured-bass information on pages 44–45. Then realize the figured basses below by following these steps:

   a. Provide the roman numerals specified by the figured bass.

   b. Compose a simple melody that will conform to the progression and at the same time will create a good counterpoint with the bass.

   c. Make two completed versions of each, one for three parts and one for four parts.

1 Three parts

B♭:

Four parts

B♭:

2 Three parts (The horizontal line beneath the last measure means that the 3rd above the bass should be retained in the next chord.)

e:

Four parts

e:

I. a. Review the chord diagrams on page 105.

b. Assign roman numerals to each of the bass notes in the following exercises, using triads (only) in root position and first inversion to create a good tonal progression.

c. Follow steps b and c for Part H. If possible, these settings should be for vocal or instrumental combinations found in your class.

Name_____ Class_____ Date_____

J. a. Select roman numerals with which to harmonize this melody, changing chords every place there is a blank. Be sure your progression is a good one.

b. Write out the melody with a bass line, using first-inversion triads where appropriate. Make sure that the bass creates a good counterpoint with the melody and that there are no objectionable parallels.

c. Make a piano setting using the bass line you composed. Keep the piano texture simple, perhaps like that in Example 8-3 (p. 115).

Chapter 9

TRIADS IN SECOND INVERSION

EXERCISE 9-1

A. Analysis. In addition to the specific instructions for each example, label each six-four chord by type.

   1. Label all chords with roman numerals. Don't forget to identify the types of six-four chords that you encounter.

 Clementi, Sonatina op. 36, no. 1, II

2. Label the chords with roman numerals, and put parentheses around all nonchord tones.

 Clara Wieck Schumann, Scherzo op. 15, no. 4

Published 1976 by Willy Müller-Süddeutscher Verlag and 1994 by Breitkopf & Härtel.

3. Label the chords with roman numerals. As before, identify the type of any six-four chord you encounter.

 Haydn, Symphony no. 100, I

4. Label the chords with roman numerals, and identify the type of any six-four chords.

Mozart, Piano Sonata, K. 331, III

5. Label the chords with roman numerals, and identify the type of any six-four chord you encounter.

Beethoven, Piano Concerto no. 1, op. 15, I

B. Fill in one or two inner parts, as specified. Identify any six-four chords by type.

C. Realize these figured basses for three or four voices, as specified, striving to create
    good outer-voice counterpoint. Notice the frequent use of $\frac{5}{3}$ (or the equivalent, such
    as $\frac{5}{\sharp}$) to indicate root-position triads following an inverted chord. Analyze with roman
    numerals, and label six-four types.

D. a. Compose a soprano line that will both fit the progression and create a good outer-voice counterpoint with the bass.

  b. Fill in alto and tenor parts to make a four-part texture.

  c. Be sure to include a six-four chord in each one, and identify the six-four type.

1

2

E. a. Harmonize each melody by composing a bass line that will create a good counterpoint with the melody and that will imply a good harmonic progression.

  b. Complete the harmonization by filling in two inner parts.

  c. Try to include an appropriate six-four chord in each harmonization.

1

G:

2

f:

F. a. Continue the accompaniment of this violin melody. Nonchord tones are in parentheses.

b. Be sure to use at least one cadential, passing, or pedal six-four chord.

c. Include a harmonic analysis.

Chapter 10

CADENCES, PHRASES, PERIODS, AND SENTENCES

EXERCISE 10-1

A. Cadences. Using only triads in root position and first inversion, compose examples of the following cadences. Each example should include three chords—the two cadence chords plus one chord preceding the cadence chords. Include key signatures and roman numerals.

1 three parts   **2** four parts   **3** three parts   **4** four parts

A: ____ ____ ____   g: ____ ____ ____   F: ____ ____ ____   b: ____ ____ ____
  (root position IAC)   (DC—careful!)   (HC)   (inverted IAC)

5 three parts   **6** four parts   **7** three parts   **8** four parts

G: ____ ____ ____   d: ____ ____ ____   B♭: ____ ____ ____   e: ____ ____ ____
  (PAC)   (PC)   (leading-tone IAC)   (Phrygian HC)

9 three parts   **10** four parts   **11** three parts   **12** four parts

a: ___ ___ ___   C: ___ ___ ___   f: ___ ___ ___   D: ___ ___ ___

   (DC—careful!)   (PAC)   (PC)   (HC)

B. Analysis. The cadence chords have been analyzed for you in each example.

  a. Make a diagram of each excerpt similar to the diagrams used in the text.

  b. Include phrase labels (a, b, and so on), and cadence types and measures.

  c. Name the form of the example.

  1. Diagram and name the form of this excerpt. Each phrase can be analyzed as a sentence. Show x and x' (with brackets) for each phrase in the score.

 Schumann, Symphony no. 1, op. 38, III (piano reduction)

2. Diagram and name the form of this excerpt. Then complete the following:

a. Diagram and name the form of mm. 1–8; then diagram and name the form of mm. 9–16.

b. Find the best example of imitation between the melody and the bass.

c. Label the chords implied by the two voices. Nonchord tones are in parentheses in the bass (only). Note: The best choice for m. 5 is *not* a ii chord. (Compare m. 5 with m. 13.)

Anonymous: Minuet in G, from the *Notebook for Anna Magdalena Bach*

3. Diagram and name the form of this three-phrase excerpt. How would you explain the descending chords in mm. 3–4 and 7–8?

Haydn, Piano Sonata no. 49, I

4. Diagram and name the form of this excerpt, and copy out any rhythmic motives found in both of the phrases. The progression at *x* resembles an IAC in what key? What is the relationship between that key and e minor?

 Mendelssohn, *Song without Words* op. 62, no. 3

5. This excerpt contains three phrases (some would call it a phrase group). Would it be better to consider it (a) a three-phrase sentence, (b) a period with two antecedent phrases, or (c) a period with two consequent phrases? Why? Which phrase features a circle-of-fifths sequence? Analyze all the chords in that phrase, and diagram the form of the excerpt.

Mozart, Piano Sonata, K. 545, I

V^7 I

6. Diagram the form of this excerpt in four ways, all of which are possible interpretations: (a) all four-measure phrases: 4 + 4 + 4 + 4 + 4; (b) four phrases, the last one extended: 4 + 4 + 4 + 8; (c) two long phrases plus a short final phrase: 8 + 8 + 4; and (d) two phrases, the second extended: 8 + 12. Which interpretation do you prefer? Why?

 Mozart, Piano Sonata, K. 310, III

84   *Tonal Harmony*

7. Diagram and name the form of this theme, and then label the first five chords. Also, see if you can find a disguised sequence hidden in the soprano and another in the bass in mm. 1–8.

Beethoven, Piano Sonata op. 13, II

C. Review. Notate the chords in the keys and bass positions indicated.

E: I^6 B♭: vi^7 G: IV^6_4 D: ii^4_3 f: VI d: $\text{vii}°^6_5$ A♭: iii E♭: $\text{vii}ø^7$ f♯: V^4_2 A: IV^{M7}

Chapter 11

TWO-PART TONAL COUNTERPOINT

EXERCISE 11-1

A. Compose bass lines to the following progressions, inverting harmonies and changing chord labels as necessary. Follow the suggested procedures and explain your decisions.

For example, given:

Here is the example with mandatory root-position pitches shown:

And again with mandatory first-inversion pitches also shown:

1. This example starts on beat 3. Begin and end the example with a half note.

B♭:   I   V   I   ii   V   vi   I   IV   V   I

2. This example starts on beat 3. Begin and end the example with a half note.

a: V   i   viiº   i   iv   V   VI   iv   iiº   V

EXERCISE 11-2

A. Analyze and critique each contrapuntal voice in terms of the guidelines for melodies discussed earlier in the section titled "Features of the Melodic Line." To avoid cluttering up the score, label the errors using the numbered list given in that section. (For example, for an improperly resolved leading tone, place the label "#7" above the location of the error.) If the errors are general and apply to the entire example, place the number to the left of the score. If the error occurs over a range of notes, show this with an additional bracket or circle.

1. D minor

2. B♭ major

EXERCISE 11-3

A. Compose a good one-to-one counterpoint to the following bass line. You may either write a PAC or a root-position IAC as the final cadence. Indicate the harmonic intervals formed by the two voices.

d: i   ii°⁶   V   i⁶   VI   iv   V   i

B. Compose a good bass line using the root-position progression below, inverting harmonies and changing chord labels as necessary. Then, compose a good one-to-one counterpoint above the bass line. Use an HC for the final cadence. The example starts on beat 3. Begin and end the example with a half note. Indicate the harmonic intervals formed by the two voices.

D: V   I   viiº   I   IV   V   I   V

C. Compose a good bass line using the two-phrase root-position progression below, inverting harmonies as necessary. Then, compose a good one-to-one counterpoint above the bass line. Use an HC to end the first phrase and a PAC to end the second phrase. The final chord of each phrase should be a whole note. Note that you do not have to preserve good voice leading over the break between the two phrases. (For example, the second phrase can begin with pitches that are disjunct in relation to the previous phrase.)

a: i   viiº   i   V   VI   iv   V

a: i   VI   iv   i   iiº   V   i

D. Invent a harmonic progression in half notes (except for the final pitch, which should be a whole note when the progression begins on beat 1) following the instructions below. Then, compose a good bass line and add a good one-to-one counterpoint above that bass line.

1. E minor, one five-measure phrase in 4/4 meter

2. F major, one four-measure phrase in 4/4 meter with a half-note pickup

3. A major, two four-measure phrases with cadences appropriate for a period in $\frac{4}{4}$ meter

4. G minor, two four-measure phrases with cadences appropriate for a period in $\frac{4}{4}$ meter

Chapter 12

NONCHORD TONES 1

EXERCISE 12-1

A. Embellish the one-to-one counterpoint given below. Indicate the harmonic intervals formed by the two voices; then underline the strong-beat labels, and put parentheses around all dissonant pitches.

B. Compose a good one-to-one counterpoint for the progression given below, inverting harmonies and changing chord labels as necessary. Then, on a different staff, compose an embellished version of that counterpoint with passing tones and arpeggiations. Add labels and parentheses as described above.

One-to-one version:

Embellished version:

Bb: V   I   vi   ii   V   I   V   I

C. Make up a progression with the parameters given below. Then, compose a good one-to-one counterpoint. Finally, on a different staff, compose an embellished version. Add labels and parentheses as described on the previous page.

1. A two-phrase period in C minor and a $\frac{4}{4}$ meter, with the two phrases ending with a root-position IAC and a PAC, respectively.

2. A two-phrase period in G major and a $\frac{4}{4}$ meter, with the two phrases ending with a HC and a root-position IAC, respectively.

EXERCISE 12-2

A. Analysis.

1. Go back to Example 8-20 (p. 126), which shows NCTs in parentheses, and identify in the following blanks the type of each NCT found in the solo horn part. Always show the interval classification (4–3 and so on) when you analyze suspensions.

m. 6 _____   m. 7 _____ _____   m. 8 _____ _____

m. 10 _____   m. 11 _____ _____

2. a. Analyze the chords and NCTs in this excerpt.

b. Make a reduction by (1) removing all NCTs, (2) using longer note values or ties for repeated notes, and (3) transposing parts by a P8 where necessary to make the lines smoother.

c. Study the simplified texture. Do any voice-leading problems appear to have been covered up by the embellishments?

d. Discuss the reasons for the leap in the tenor in m. 3.

 Bach, "Hilf, Herr Jesu, lass gelingen"

Reduction

B. After reviewing Suspensions and Retardations on pages 195–205, decide what *one* suspension would be best in each excerpt that follows. Then, renotate with that suspension and at least one other embellishment. Remember to put parentheses around NCTs and to label NCTs and arpeggiations.

b: V⁶ i ii°⁶ V   A: IV⁶ I V I⁶   g: i iv i⁶ vii°⁶   E♭: IV V⁶ I V⁶

C. The following example is a simplified excerpt from a Bach chorale harmonization. Label the chords with roman numerals and activate the texture with stepwise NCTs, including at least one suspension. Label all embellishments.

B♭:

D. In the figured basses that follow, the symbols "4 #" call for a 4–3 suspension, with a
    sharp applied to the note of resolution. The symbols "6 –" indicate that a first inversion
    triad is to be used above both Cs in the bass.

For each figured bass, do the following:

1. Analyze the harmonies with roman numerals.

2. Compose a simple but musical soprano line.

3. Fill in one or two inner parts, as specified.

4. Add some stepwise NCTs to each example and label them.

1

a:

2

g:

E. a. Using the following progressions, compose a good soprano/bass framework, using inversions where desired.

b. Add one or two inner parts, as specified.

c. Show with an *x* every possible location for a 9–8, 7–6, 4–3, or 2–3 suspension.

d. Create an elaborated version of the simple texture, including at least one suspension. Other embellishments should be limited to arpeggiations and stepwise NCTs.

1. Three-part texture. (Remember that diminished triads should be used in first inversion.)

2. Four-part texture.

F.   Compose your own harmonic progression and follow the instructions for Part E. Try a two, three, or four-part texture.

G. Analyze the chords implied by this two-voice framework. Then, embellish the framework in an arrangement for string quartet. A suggested beginning is given.

H. Continue your solution to Part G to form a parallel period.

Chapter 13

NONCHORD TONES 2

EXERCISE 13-1

A. Analysis.

1. Go back to Example 7-17 on page 104 of the text, where NCTs are shown in parentheses, and identify the type of each NCT in the following blanks. Always show the interval classification (7–6 and so on) when you analyze suspensions.

    m. 1 _____ _____   m. 3 _____ _____

2. Do the same for Example 10-14 on pages 156–157 of the text.

    m. 10 _____   m. 11 _____   m. 13 _____

    m. 14 _____   m. 15 _____   m. 16, violin: _____   m. 16, piano: _____ _____

3. Do the same for Example 9-12 on page 140.

    VI. I: m. 23 _____   m. 24 _____   m. 25 _____   m. 26 _____

    VI. II: m. 23 _____   m. 26 _____ _____ _____

4. Label chords and NCTs in this excerpt.

 Mozart, Piano Sonata, K. 545, II

G: _____

5. The chords in this excerpt have been labeled for you. Put parentheses around all NCTs in mm. 1–6 (only), and label them. The roman numerals in parentheses are part of a "nonfunctional" series of parallel sixth chords (review pp. 118–120), and some other chords have been left unlabeled because they are too advanced for you at this point. The last three measures are included for context, but they are not part of this exercise.

 Clara Wieck Schumann, Larghetto, op. 15, no. 1

6. NCTs in jazz and popular melodies tend to be used in ways that are not typical of music of earlier centuries. See if you can identify some instances here.

 Davis, "Little Willy Leaps"

B. Using a three-part texture, write authentic cadences in five different keys, employing a different NCT from the following list in each cadence: p, n, ant, app, e. Use three chords in each example.

C. a. Analyze the chords in this phrase with roman numerals.

   b. Renotate the phrase on the following staves, adding at least four NCTs, at least two of which should be suspensions.

   c. Label all the NCTs, and show the interval classifications of the suspensions.

D. Compose a simple melody for each figured bass below and fill in inner voices to make a four-part texture. Include some of the NCTs studied in this chapter. Analyze chords and NCTs.

In this example, use a V chord on beat 3 of m. 1. Also, the symbols "6 – –" mean that a first inversion chord is to be maintained throughout m. 2.

2

F:

E. Compose a passage in four parts in the key of b minor, employing a 7–6 suspension near the beginning and a tonic pedal near the end.

F. Compose eight measures to continue Part A, number 3, on page 72 of this workbook. Maintain a similar texture and end with a PAC. Include an NCT studied in this chapter.

G. The following framework is a simplified version of a passage from Mozart's *The Magic Flute*. Embellish the framework, turning it into a vocal part (to be sung on neutral syllables) with piano accompaniment. Try to include at least one chromatic NCT.

H. Continue your solution to Part G to form a parallel period.

Chapter 14

Part III

Diatonic Seventh Chords

THE V⁷ CHORD

EXERCISE 14-1

A. The note given in each case is the root, 3rd, 5th, or 7th of a V⁷ chord. Notate the chord in root position, and name the major key in which it would be the V⁷.

B. Analyze chords and NCTs in the following excerpt, including roman numerals and lead-sheet symbols. Then, discuss the voice leading in the two V⁷ chords. (Note: You might have analyzed the Bs in the V chords as passing tones, but consider them to be chord 7ths for the purposes of your discussion.)

Bach, "Wir Christenleut'"

C. Resolve each chord to a root-position I. (Note: *c* means complete chord, *i* means incomplete chord.)

D. Notate the key signature and the V⁷ chord, and then resolve it.

1 three parts   **2** three parts   **3** four parts   **4** four parts   **5** four parts

G: V^7 I   d: V^7 i   E: V^7 I   A♭: V^7 I   f♯: V^7 i
                                       (c)   (i)   (c)   (c)   (i)   (c)

6 three parts   **7** three parts   **8** four parts   **9** four parts   **10** four parts

E♭: V^7 vi   A: V^7 vi   f: V^7 VI   b♭: V^7 VI   D: V^7 vi

E. Analyze the chords specified by this figured bass, using roman numerals and lead-sheet symbols. Then, make two harmonizations: one for SAB chorus and one for SATB chorus.

F. Analyze the chords implied by the following soprano and bass lines. Then, fill in the inner parts. Remember that the tenor part sounds a P8 lower than written.

G. Analyze the harmonies implied by these soprano/bass frameworks. Then, make four-
   part versions with embellishments and at least one root-position V⁷ chord.

1

2

3

H. Set a short text for four-part chorus. The text might be a poem, a headline from a news-
    paper, or anything. Include at least one V⁷–I progression. Try to keep the motion going
    through the use of elaborations.

I. Compose a period in a simple three-part texture. End the first phrase with a V^7–vi DC, the second with a V^7–I PAC. Then, create a version for three instruments, the top part being elaborated by arpeggiations and NCTs, the other two parts in an accompanying role. Turn in both versions.

1. Simple version

2. Elaborated version

EXERCISE 14-2

A. Notate the specified chords. Use accidentals instead of key signatures.

1	2	3	4	5	6	7	8

D♭: V$^6_5$ a: V$^4_3$ E♭: V$^4_2$ D: V$^4_3$ c: V$^4_2$ F: V$^6_5$ b: V$^4_2$ E: V$^6_5$

B. Label chords and NCTs in the following excerpts. Comment on the treatment of the leading tone and 7th in any V^7 chords in root position or inversion.

Notice that in Exercises 1 and 3, the key signature does not agree with the given key. This is because in each case the music has modulated (changed key) to the dominant. Modulation will be introduced in Chapter 18.

1. Bach, "Ich dank' dir, lieber Herre"

(Which is the more sensible analysis of beat 4 of m. 3: iii$^6_4$ or V^6?)

F:

2. Beethoven, Piano Sonata op. 2, no. 1, III

3. Mozart, Quintet for Piano and Winds K. 452, I

Bb:

4. Schumann, "Im Westen," op. 25, no. 23

(Do not label NCTs in this excerpt.)

mich   und mein   Kind - lein   an's   Herz _____ ged - rückt.

*Name*_____ *Class*_____ *Date*_____

C. Resolve each chord to a tonic triad (except as indicated). Analyze both chords.

D. Notate, introduce, and resolve the specified chords. Each chord 7th is to be approached as indicated. Include key signatures, lead-sheet symbols with slash symbols, and roman numerals.

Eb: _____ V^6_5 _____ g: _____ V^4_2 _____ D: _____ V^7 _____ b: _____ V^4_3 _____

G: _____ V^7 vi f: _____ V^6_5 _____ Bb: _____ V^7 _____ c#: _____ V^4_3 i6

E: _____ V^7 _____ c: _____ V^4_2 _____ Ab: _____ V^4_3 I f#: _____ V^7 VI

E. Show with lead-sheet symbols and roman numerals the chords that this figured bass
   calls for. Then, complete the realization in four voices.

F. Analyze with roman numerals the chords implied by each soprano/bass framework.
    Then, add inner parts and embellishments to make a four-part choral texture. Include
    an inverted V^7 chord.

G. Analyze the chords implied by this soprano/bass framework. Then, create a piano texture by filling out some of the chords and adding embellishments. Arpeggiations will be especially useful for prolonging the I chord in mm. 1–2. Be sure to include an inverted V^7 chord.

H. Make one or more settings of the following song.

1. Write an arrangement for two B♭ trumpets, unaccompanied. Analyze the harmonies implied by the two lines. Include at least one inverted V^7.

2. Make an arrangement for four-part chorus. Try to elaborate the other voices slightly. Include at least one inverted V^7. Watch out for parallel 8ves and 5ths throughout.

3. Compose a version for piano solo, including at least one inverted V^7. Be prepared to play it, or find someone else in the class who will do so.

I. Compose a period for a string trio (violin, viola, cello) or for some other combination of instruments in your class. Include at least two inverted V^7 chords.

Chapter 15

OTHER DIATONIC SEVENTH CHORDS

EXERCISE 15-1

A. Notate the following chords. Use accidentals, not key signatures.

B. Analyze the following chords. Be sure your symbols indicate chord quality and inversion.

C. Analyze the chords in the following excerpts. Comment on the voice leading involving any of the chords discussed in this chapter.

 1. Bach, "Herzliebster Jesu, was hast du verbrochen"

b:

 2. Bach, "Herr Jesu Christ, du höchstes Gut"

3. Corelli, Concerto Grosso op. 6, no. 1, VII

D: iii

4. Haydn, Piano Sonata no. 30, I

After you finish labeling all the chords, complete the three-part reduction of mm. 86–92 that follows the excerpt. The neighbor figures in 16th notes in mm. 84–91 are NCTs, not the sevenths of chords.

f#:

Textural reduction

5. Haydn, String Quartet op. 50, no. 6, II

Label the chords in the blanks provided. Do not label NCTs in this excerpt.
The *m.v.* dynamic markings stand for *mezza voce*, "half voice," which means
approximately the same thing as *mezzo forte*, or *mf*. The tempo is *Poco Adagio*.

Name_____ Class_____ Date_____

D. Notate, introduce, and resolve the specified chords. Approach each chord 7th as a suspension, a neighbor, or a passing tone, as specified. Include key signatures, lead-sheet symbols with slash symbols, and roman numerals.

F: ___ iii⁷ ___   E: ___ IVᴹ ₅⁶ ___   g: ___ i ₅⁶ ___   b: ___ #vi°⁷ ___

f: ___ vii°⁷ ___   c#: ___ iv ₃⁴ ___   a: ___ iiø ₅⁶ ___   D: ___ vi⁷ ___

G: ___ ₅⁶ IVᴹ ₂⁴ ___ ₅⁶   c: ___ ⁷ VIᴹ ₃⁴ ___ ⁷   B♭: ___ ⁷ Iᴹ⁷ ___ ⁷   d: ___ IV ₅⁶ ___
   (circle of fifths)   (circle of fifths)   (circle of fifths)

E. Continue this three-part elaboration of a circle-of-fifths sequence.

f: iv⁷   VII⁷   IIIᴹ⁷   VIᴹ⁷   iiø⁷   V⁷   i

F. Analyze the chords called for by the figured bass that follows. Remember that the figured-bass symbols are part of the music, not part of the harmonic analysis, which should be written beneath it. Then, continue the four-part realization of that figured bass. Note: Be sure to review pages 249–250 before proceeding. (Figures in the fifth measure added by the authors.)

Corelli, Concerto Grosso op. 6, no. 12, V

Realization

F: I   IV^M7   vii°7

G. Analyze this figured bass and continue the realization, keeping the keyboard texture but following conventional part-writing procedures.

Corelli, Concerto Grosso, op. 6, no. 9, "Preludio"

H. Compose a passage for three voices or instruments containing a sequence of seventh chords similar to that used in the excerpt of Part F.

I. The following is a simple note-against-note contrapuntal framework. Analyze the implied harmonies, and then elaborate it into a passage containing several seventh chords. Use four parts or a free keyboard texture. Your final version might be complex, but the original framework should be retained. Include roman numerals and NCT analysis.

J. Create a framework similar to Exercise I but in the minor mode. Be sure it implies a good harmonic progression. Then, create an elaboration that employs some of the seventh chords discussed in this chapter. If possible, score for a combination of instruments in your class.

Chapter 16

Part IV
Chromaticism 1

SECONDARY FUNCTIONS 1

EXERCISE 16-1

A. Review the material on spelling secondary dominants (p. 258). Then, notate these secondary dominants in the specified inversions. Include key signatures and lead-sheet symbols without slash symbols.

1	2	3	4	5
c#: V^7/iv	A♭: V^6/V	c: V$^4_3$/VI	e: V^6/III	F: V$^4_2$/ii

6	7	8	9	10
D: V^6/vi	b: V^7/V	A: V$^6_5$/iii	g: V/iv	a: V$^4_2$/V

11	12	13	14	15
E♭: V$^6_5$/IV	f#: V^6/VII	C: V^7/ii	B♭: V$^4_2$/IV	G: V$^4_3$/V

B. Label with a roman numeral any chord that might be a secondary dominant according to the steps outlined on pages 258–259. Label all others with an *x*.

f: _____   E: _____   C: _____   e: _____   g: _____

Eb: _____   f#: _____   D: _____   F: _____   c: _____

A: _____   b: _____   d: _____   Bb: _____   G: _____

EXERCISE 16-2

A. Analysis.

1. Label chords and NCTs. Identify any six-four chords by type. This excerpt contains a set of parallel 5ths in a context that Bach must have found acceptable because he used them so often in this situation. See if you can find them.

  Bach, "Freuet euch, ihr Christen alle"

f:

2. Label the chords with roman numerals. There are a few sequences in this excerpt. Find two and bracket them.

  Kuhlau, Sonatina op. 88, no. 2, II

3. Analyze with roman numerals the chords called for by these lead-sheet symbols, referring to Appendix B if necessary. Then, continue the accompaniment, keeping the four-part texture and using conventional voice leading. It may be helpful to review Example 16-7 on page 260 before you begin.

Fields and Kern, "Pick Yourself Up"

F:

4. Label chords and NCTs. Ignore the grace notes in your harmonic and NCT analysis; for example, the E♭5 in m. 1 is an upper neighbor ornamented by the appoggiatura grace note. Comment on Chopin's use of F♯ and F♮ in this excerpt. Where do they occur? Are they ever in conflict? The form of the excerpt is a (parallel/contrasting) (period/double period).

 Chopin, Mazurka op. 67, no. 2

5. Label chords and NCTs. What is the form of this excerpt? (Note: Measures 1–2 are introductory.)

  Beethoven, String Quartet op. 135, III

6. Label the chords with roman numerals. Label NCTs in the solo bassoon part only. The note under the fermata in m. 49 represents a V chord. It was at this point that the soloist improvised a cadenza. The conductor waited until he heard the soloist arrive at the G3 (often trilled), at which point he would signal the orchestra to be ready for its entrance in m. 50.

Mozart, Bassoon Concerto K. 191, II

B. For each of the following problems, first analyze the given chord. Next, find a smooth way to lead into the chord. Although there are many possibilities, it will often work to use a chord whose root is a P5 above the root of the secondary dominant. Experiment with other relationships also. Then, resolve each chord properly, taking special care with the leading tone and 7th resolutions. Analyze all chords with roman numerals and lead-sheet symbols without slash symbols.

C. List below each note the secondary V and V⁷ chords that could harmonize that note. You might find it helpful to refer to Examples 16-3 and 16-4 on page 257.

D. Provide roman numerals to show how the first note could be harmonized as a second-
    ary dominant. The second note should be a member of the tonicized triad.

g: F: b: f: E:

c: C: B♭:   e: A:

E. Analyze the chords specified by each figured bass, putting your analysis *beneath* the
    figures. Then, make an arrangement for SATB chorus. Strive for smooth voice leading,
    even if this results in a dull soprano line.

Name_____ Class_____ Date_____

F. Harmonize each chorale phrase for SATB chorus. Include one or more secondary dominants in each phrase and activate the texture with some NCTs.

1

E♭:

2

d:

3

C:

4

g:

G. Analyze the harmonies implied by the following soprano/bass framework. Then, make
    a more interesting version for piano, beginning with the two measures given in the
    example that follows.

H. Continue the following example to make a total of at least eight measures. Include one
    or more secondary dominants and end with a PAC. Then, score it for four instruments
    found in your class. Analyze all chords and NCTs.

I. Finish the analysis of the following phrase. This phrase is to serve as the *a* phrase of a longer theme you will compose. The theme will be in the form of a parallel double period. Include at least one secondary dominant.

A: (I)   (V^7)   I

Chapter 17

SECONDARY FUNCTIONS 2

EXERCISE 17-1

A. Review how to spell secondary leading-tone chords (pp. 274–275). Then, notate these secondary leading-tone chords in the specified inversion. Include key signatures.

1	2	3	4	5
A: vii°6/iii	F: vii°6/ii	c: vii°6/VI	E: vii°6/5/IV	A♭: vii°7/IV

6	7	8	9	10
d: vii°6/5/V	G: vii°7/vi	B♭: vii°6/vi	g: vii°7/VII	F: vii°7/ii

11	12	13	14	15
C: vii⌀4/2/V	e: vii°6/iv	E♭: vii⌀4/3/V	f♯: vii°7/III	D: vii°6/V

B. Label any chord that would be a secondary leading-tone chord according to the steps outlined on page 275. Label all others with an *x*.

1
c: _____

2
G: _____

3
A: _____

4
B♭: _____

5
e: _____

6
C: _____

7
d: _____

8
E: _____

9
E♭: _____

10
A♭: _____

11
F: _____

12
f♯: _____

13
D: _____

14
C: _____

15
c♯: _____

Name_____ Class_____ Date_____

EXERCISE 17-2

A. Analysis.

1. In the brilliant and witty concluding passage that follows, Mozart combines the antecedent and consequent phrases from the beginning of the minuet (marked *a* and *b* in mm. 55–58).

   a. Mark all occurrences of *a* and *b*.

   b. Find where *b* is used in imitation.

   c. Find inverted (upside down) statements of *a* and *b*.

   d. Find a place where original and inverted statements of *b* are used simultaneously.

   e. Put roman numerals in the blanks provided. NCTs are in parentheses.

Mozart, String Quartet K. 464, II

2. Listen carefully to this excerpt, and then put roman numerals in the blanks provided. The B♭ in the ii°$^4_3$ chord in m. 6 is "borrowed" from the parallel minor; borrowed chords are discussed in Chapter 21.

Dussek, Piano Sonata op. 69, no. 3, I

Allegro maestoso e brillante

D: I   _____   _____   _____   ii°$^4_3$

3. Label the chords with roman numerals (the Italian augmented sixth chord in m. 4 will be discussed in Chapter 22). Use your imagination and your ear in analyzing the last chord in m. 2.

Schumann, "Die Löwenbraut," op. 31, no. 1

4. Label chords and NCTs. (An optional piano accompaniment is omitted from the example.) In the penultimate chord, assume that the bass note is the B3, even though the first alto is below it with an A3. What is the form of this excerpt?

 Brahms, "Und gehst du über den Kirchhof," op. 44, no. 10

5. Analyze chords and NCTs. Find two circle-of-fifths progressions that contain more than four chords. What is the form of this excerpt?

Tchaikovsky, "Morning Prayer," op. 39, no. 1

6. This short song is given here in its entirety.

   a. Analyze the chords and NCTs. There are some places where alternative analyses are possible—in m. 1, for example, where the line G♯–F♯–E could be analyzed as chord tones or as passing tones.

   b. Think of two analyses for the second chord in m. 11, one of them being a secondary function.

Schumann, "Aus meinen Thränen spriessen," op. 48, no. 2

Name_____ Class_____ Date_____

B. For each of these problems, first analyze and resolve the given chord, being especially careful with the chord 7th and the leading tone. Then, find a smooth way to lead into the given chord. Analyze all chords with roman numerals and lead-sheet symbols without slash symbols.

C: ___ ___ ___   D: ___ ___ ___   A: ___ ___ ___   Eb: ___ ___ ___   Bb: ___ ___ ___

E: ___ ___ ___   c: ___ ___ ___   f: ___ ___ ___   g: ___ ___ ___   F: ___ ___ ___

C. Analyze the harmonies specified by each figured bass and make an arrangement for SATB chorus. Try to use smooth voice leading, even at the expense of an interesting soprano line.

2

4+ 6   4   6   6   6   6♮   6   7
2   2   5♭   5   4   #

D. Harmonize each of these chorale phrases for SATB chorus. Include at least one secondary leading-tone chord or incorporate some other aspect discussed in this chapter in each harmonization.

1

F:

a:

3

F:

Name _____ Class _____ Date _____

E. Each item that follows contains two versions of the same excerpt, one of them in a sim-
    ple texture and one more elaborate. Continue the simple texture first, including some
    aspect of harmony discussed in this chapter. Then continue the elaboration, using your
    simple version as a framework. Label chords and NCTs.

1a.

1b.

2a.

2b.

F. Below is the harmonic progression from "St. Thomas," a jazz standard by Sonny
    Rollins. (Other versions of the progression also exist, which is not uncommon for jazz
    tunes.) Continue the piano accompaniment using conventional voice leading. As a
    bonus, listen to the Sonny Rollins performance (Jazz Hour B000T97XNE), and notate
    the melody on the top staff.

Chapter 18

MODULATIONS USING DIATONIC COMMON CHORDS

EXERCISE 18-1

A. Name the relative key in each case.

1. G♭ _____

2. A _____

3. e _____

4. g _____

5. C♯ _____

6. d _____

7. F♯ _____

8. c♯ _____

9. A♭ _____

10. a♭ _____

B. Name all the keys closely related to the given key. Be sure to use uppercase for major, lowercase for minor.

1. b _____ _____ _____ _____ _____

2. e♭ _____ _____ _____ _____ _____

3. G _____ _____ _____ _____ _____

4. B _____ _____ _____ _____ _____

5. F _____ _____ _____ _____ _____

6. f♯ _____ _____ _____ _____ _____

C. Name the relationship in each case (enharmonically equivalent, parallel, relative and closely related, closely related, foreign).

1. D/e _____

2. e♭/G♭ _____

3. A/a _____

4. d♯/G _____

5. B♭/F _____

6. A♭/C♭ _____

7. C♯/D♭ _____

8. g♯/c♯ _____

9. a♭/b♭ _____

10. c/E♭ _____

EXERCISE 18-2

A. Analysis.

1. This excerpt modulates from B♭ to F, its dominant. The blanks beneath the music show where the bass changes but do not indicate the location of the common chord. NCTs in mm. 1 and 8 (only) have been identified for you. Begin by supplying lead-sheet symbols without slashes above the staff, and then provide the roman numerals.

Szymanowska, Nocturne

B♭:

2. a Label chords and NCTs in this chorale, which is presented in its entirety.

b. Which two phrases are very similar melodically?

c. What portion of these phrases is harmonized similarly?

d. What chord is emphasized in the first half of the second of these two phrases?

Bach, "Uns ist ein Kindlein heut' geborn"

3. This example, also a complete chorale, is in g minor, although it ends with a major triad (the "Picardy third").

   a. Label chords, but not the NCTs.

   b. Notice how often the melody follows an arch contour (inverted in the second phrase). Bracket those arch contours in the melody.

   c. If you find any similar contours in the bass, bracket them also.

 Bach, "Jesu, der du meine Seele"

4. Label the chords with roman numerals. How do the pickup notes at the beginning of the excerpt help smooth the return to the first key when the repeat is taken?

Mozart, Piano Sonata K. 330, II

5. Label the chords with roman numerals.

Fanny Mendelssohn Hensel, "Das Meer erglänzte weit hinaus."

wir __ sas - sen am ein - sa-men Fi - scher - haus, wir __

sas - sen __ stumm und al - lei - ne.

6. a. Listen to this song all the way through. Then, list every tonality that is touched on in the song, either by simple tonicization or by modulation.

    b. Which (other than tonic) is referred to again at the end of the song?

    c. Decide on one or two tonalities (other than tonic) that represent modulations rather than tonicizations.

    d. Label all chords with roman numerals.

 Schumann, "Wenn ich in deine Augen seh'," op. 48, no. 4

7. This excerpt begins in A♭ and ends in g minor, modulating through yet another key in the process. Label all chords, and label the NCTs in the vocal part. The German augmented sixth chord in m. 49 will be discussed in Chapter 22.

Mozart, Marriage of Figaro, K. 492, "Voi che sapete"

8. Label the chords with roman numerals. In an Alberti bass accompaniment, such as the left hand in this example, the bass note for each chord is usually considered to be the lowest note struck. So in m. 9 the only *bass* notes are D and C♯.

  Beethoven, Piano Sonata op. 10, no. 3, II

B. Fill in the name of the new key on the second line of each exercise.

1. e: i   ii°6   V$_2^4$ i6   iv6

                  ____ :   i6   V$_2^4$ i6   ii°6   V^7 i

2. D: I   V   I6   vii°6

              ____ :   ii°6   i$_4^6$ V   i

                                  V

3. F: I   vii°6   I6   vi

              ____ :   ii   vii°6   I   V$_5^6$ I

4. g: i   V$_5^6$ V$_2^4$/iv   iv6   V   i6

                        ____ :   iv6   ii°6   V^7 i

5. b: i   ii°$_2^4$ V$_5^6$ i   VI   iv6

                        ____ :   ii6   I$_4^6$ V^7 I

                                      V

6. E♭:   I   ii6   V   vi

              ____ :   iv   ii°$_5^6$ V   VI   iv   V   i

7. A: I   V$_3^4$ I6   V6

              ____ :   IV6   V$_5^6$ i   ii°$_5^6$ i$_4^6$ V^7 i

                                        V

8. c: i   V^7 VI   iv

              ____ :   vi   IV6   (I$_4^6$)   ii$_5^6$ V   I

C. List the diatonic triads that could serve as common chords between each pair of keys. In minor keys, assume the usual chord qualities: i, ii°, III, iv, V, VI, vii°.

ex. First key, C: I   iii   V   vi
   Triads: C   Em   G   Am
   Second key, G: IV   vi   I   ii

1. First key, E:
   Triads:
   Second key, f♯:

2. First key, D♭:
   Triads:
   Second key, G♭:

3. First key, c:
   Triads:
   Second key, B♭:

4. First key, f:
   Triads:
   Second key, A♭:

5. First key, B:
   Triads:
   Second key, F♯:

6. First key, A♭:
   Triads:
   Second key, B♭:

D. Choose two of the progressions from Part B. Arrange one for SATB chorus and the other for SAB chorus. Activate the texture with NCTs and/or arpeggiations. Arrange the metric and rhythmic structure so that the last chord comes on a strong beat. Label chords and NCTs.

E. Harmonize the following chorale tunes for SATB chorus.

1. In the first phrase, modulate from i to III. The second phrase should return to i.

2. Modulate from I to vi in phrase 1. Return to I in phrase 2.

F. Analyze the chords specified by this figured bass, and then make an arrangement for SATB chorus.

G. Continue this soprano/bass framework, analyzing the implied harmonies. Phrase 1 (mm. 1–4) should end with a HC in f. Phrase 2 (mm. 5–8) should end with a PAC in A♭. The resulting form is a modulating period. Then, arrange for some combination of instruments in your class, filling in as many inner parts as needed. Elaborate your final version with NCTs and arpeggiations.

f:　　　　　i　vii°6　　i6

H. Compose a double period for some solo instrument with piano accompaniment. As the diagram indicates, the first phrase stays in A, whereas the second tonicizes (or modulates to) E. Phrase 3 returns briefly to A but turns quickly to D. The fourth phrase returns to A for the final cadence.

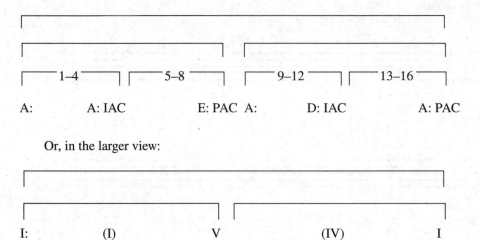

Or, in the larger view:

The beginning of phrase 1 is given next. Compose the soprano/bass framework first.

Name_____ Class_____ Date_____

I.   Using a text of your own choosing, compose a passage for chorus (three or four parts). If in major, it should have a tonal scheme of I–vi–I–ii–I. If in minor, use i–VI–i–iv–i.

Chapter 19

SOME OTHER MODULATORY TECHNIQUES

EXERCISE 19-1

A. Analysis. (Note: Some of the modulations that follow might be of the diatonic common-chord type.)

1. a. What three keys are implied in this excerpt?

   b. How would you explain the modulations?

   c. Continue the two-voice reduction below the score, but avoid the change of register in m. 36.

Beethoven, Piano Sonata op. 10, no. 1, I

Textural reduction

2. Two modulations occur in this excerpt.

   a. Label chords and NCTs.

   b. At what point does Bach not follow the conventions of spacing discussed in Chapter 5 on pages 70–72?

   c. What is achieved by the spacing he uses?

   d. Where is a sonority used in an unusual bass position?

   e. How is the reason for this bass position related to the question about the spacing?

    Bach, "Warum betrübst du dich"

3. What two keys are found in this excerpt? How are they related? What is the best way to describe the modulation? Label the chords with roman numerals.

Hüllmandel, "*Un Poco Adagio*"

4. Two distantly related keys are found in this passage. Label chords and (in the voice only) NCTs.

Mozart, Don Giovanni, "Deh vieni alla finestra"

5. This excerpt modulates from F major to what other key? Of excerpts 1 through 4, which modulation most closely resembles this one? In what ways? It is not necessary to label all of the chords. (The chords in mm. 35–36 are labeled for you because some of them involve concepts discussed in later chapters.)

Mozart, Marriage of Figaro, K. 492, "Voi che sapete"

Sen - to un af - fet - to pien de de - sir, ____

Ch'o - ra è di - let - to, ch'o - ra è mar - tir.

i   Ger+6   V

Ge - lo, e poi sen - to l'al - ma av-vam - par,

B. Analyze the harmonies implied by this soprano/bass framework. Add an alto part to create a three-part texture. Embellish the texture with a few NCTs, including a 4–3 suspension. Identify the modulatory technique used.

C. Analyze the implied harmonies and then add alto and tenor parts. Enliven the texture with NCTs and/or arpeggiations. Identify the modulatory technique used.

D. Use the framework that follows as the basis for a repeated period. The second phrase should begin and end in D major (phrase modulation). Compose a first ending that modulates back to F using some modulatory technique discussed in this chapter. Include NCTs and arpeggiations in your final version. Score for piano or some combination of instruments found in your class.

E. The framework that follows is also to be used as the basis for a repeated period for piano (or other instruments). The first phrase is in E♭, and the second should be a sequential repetition of the first, in A♭. Write out the repeat of phrases 1 to 2. Use more embellishments in the repeat than you used in the first eight measures.

Chapter 20

LARGER FORMS

EXERCISE 20-1

A. Diagram this excerpt down to the phrase level and name the form. Assume all phrases are four measures long. Answer the following questions as well:

1. What is the form of mm. 1–8?

2. Find and label a vii°$^4_3$/V and a vii°$^4_3$/vi.

3. Why do you think Mozart chose to use a double stop in the violas in m. 7? (A double stop is a technique that allows a stringed instrument to play two notes at once.)

 Mozart, *Eine kleine Nachtmusik*, III

B. Name the form of this piece (do not diagram phrases and cadences). Watch out for written-out repeats. Also, do or answer the following:

1. Label the chords in mm. 5–8.

2. What chord forms the basis of mm. 33–39?

3. Analyze the last chord in m. 34.

4. In what measures does the "boom-chick-chick" accompaniment drop out?

 Chopin, Mazurka op. 67, no. 3

Name_____ Class_____ Date_____

C. This excerpt is the first part of a scherzo and trio (a scherzo is much like a minuet, only faster). The trio is not shown.

1. Diagram this scherzo at the phrase level. The key implied by mm. 17–20 is d minor, not A major.

2. Identify the form. Do not be misled by the written-out repeat in mm. 9–16—this is a two-reprise form.

3. Find three examples of chromatic mediant relationships.

 Beethoven, Violin Sonata op. 24, III

D. Diagram this piece down to the phrase level and name the form. Answer the following questions as well:

1. Where is a sequence involving both hands? Bracket it.

2. What does the G#4 in m. 6 accomplish?

3. What material in mm. 10–22 is obviously derived from mm. 1–9?

March from the *Notebook for Anna Magdalena Bach*

E. This excerpt, the final movement of a piano sonata, is a minuet and trio, although Haydn did not label it as such.

1. Diagram phrases and cadences, treating the minuet and trio as separate pieces. Be sure to play or listen to the music because some of the returns are disguised. (A melodically varied return of phrase *a* is still labeled phrase *a*, not phrase *a′*.)

2. Name the forms of the minuet and the trio.

3. In performance, the trio is followed by a return to the minuet (although the repeats are omitted), ending at the fermata. What is the form of the movement as a whole?

4. Find the one phrase in this movement that is not four measures long and compare it to its earlier four-measure version. How does Haydn extend this phrase?

5. Provide roman numerals for the following chords:

    a. _____ m. 17, beats 1 to 2 (in E♭)

    b. _____ m. 19, beat 3 (in E♭)

    c. _____ m. 35, beat 3 (in A♭)

    d. _____ m. 44 (in A♭)

    e. _____ m. 46, beat 3 (in A♭)

Haydn, Piano Sonata no. 38, III

F. The following five excerpts are all taken from a piano sonata movement that can be analyzed as a sonata form. Match the number of each example with the following parts of the sonata: *primary theme, transition, secondary theme, closing section,* and *development.* Then, provide reasons for each of your answers. You should consider issues such as key, cadences, and thematic character. The home key of this movement is B♭ major.

Example 1: _____

Example 2: _____

Example 3: _____

Example 4: _____

Example 5: _____

Mozart, Piano Sonata, K. 333, I

1

2

3

4

5

G. This excerpt, the final movement of a piano sonata, is a five-part rondo. In the score, label each of the five parts as A, B, or C, as applicable, above the staff.

What is the form of the A section? _____

Beethoven, Piano Sonata op. 49, no. 2, II

Part V

Chromaticism 2

Chapter 21

MODE MIXTURE AND THE NEAPOLITAN

EXERCISE 21-1

A. Notate these chords in the specified inversions. Include key signatures.

1	2	3	4	5
A: ii⌀$^4_2$	F: vii°^{7}	D♭: i$^6_4$	C: ♭VI	E: ii°^{6}

6	7	8	9	10
c♯: N^6	E♭: iv^6	f♯: I	D: ♭III	G: N^6

B. Label the chords with lead-sheet symbols without slashes and roman numerals.

C. Analysis.

1. Label the chords, circling the roman numerals of any borrowed chords. Label the cadence type.

Brahms, Symphony no. 3, op. 90, II

2. At the end of this song, a father's frantic ride comes to an end. As a Neapolitan chord resolves, we learn that the boy in his arms is dead.

Schubert, "Erlkönig," op. 1

3. In the following passage, Mozart uses mode mixture twice to move from E major to the very distant key of c minor; he then uses mode mixture twice more to return to E major. Label all chords, including the common-chord modulations from E to c and back. (Remember that the bass voice is always the lowest-sounding voice, so the bass note in m. 221, for example, is the cello G, not the piano E♭.)

Mozart, Piano Trio K. 542, I

4. Label the chords in this modulating excerpt.

   Beethoven, Piano Sonata op. 27, no. 2, I

c♯:

5. Label the chords in this excerpt.

Schubert, String Quartet op. 168, I

6. This beautiful excerpt is from the slow introduction to the first movement of a concerto. As is often the case, the Neapolitan is reserved for a particularly dramatic moment.

 Spohr, Clarinet Concerto, op. 26, I

7. Schumann uses mode mixture in this passage to modulate from E to its minor dominant. Label all the chords and the common-chord modulation.

Schumann, "Liebeslied," op. 51, no. 5

D. For each exercise, provide the correct key signature, and notate the specified chords preceding and following the N⁶. Use the given three- or four-part texture in each case.

b: iv   N⁶   V   e: VI   N⁶ V_2^4 c: iv   N⁶ i_4^6 V   g: iv   N⁶   vii°⁷/V

                                                                               V

E. Part writing. Analyze the chords implied by the soprano/bass framework. Then, fill in the alto and tenor parts.

   1. Include a iv⁶ and a ii⁰$\frac{4}{3}$.

   2. Include a Neapolitan chord.

d:

   3. Include a Neapolitan chord.

b:

F. The first two phrases of a chorale melody are given next. A bass line is included for the first phrase. Complete the four-part texture, including in the second phrase a modulation to B♭ and a borrowed iv⁶ chord. Label all chords, and circle the roman numeral of the borrowed chord. Activate the texture with NCTs and/or arpeggiations.

G. Analyze the chords specified by this figured bass, and then make an arrangement for SATB chorus.

g: V

H. Make settings of the following progressions for three or four parts, as specified. Arrange the rhythmic/metric scheme so that the final chord of each progression comes on a strong beat. Activate the texture with arpeggiations and/or NCTs.

1. (4 parts)   g: i   V i^6 i   VI V^4_2/N N^6 vii°^{7}/V i^6_4 V   i

                                                                             V

2. (3 parts)   D: I   V I^6 vi iv^6

                             F: ii^6 V^4_2 I^6 V^6_5/V i^6_4 V   I

                                                                                        V

3. (4 parts)   F: I   vii°$^6_5$ I^6 V^6_5 I   vii°$^4_3$/IV iv^6

                                                              bb: i^6 iv i^6_4 V   i

                                                                                      V

4. (3 parts)   b: i   V   VI i^6 N^6

                             G: IV^6 V^6_5 I   V   I

I. Use the framework that follows as the first phrase of a three-phrase excerpt having the following structure:

   b: HC ⟿ f♯:   HC   PAC

Phrase 2 modulates to f♯ minor. Phrase 3 remains in f♯ minor and contains a Neapolitan triad. After completing the framework, make a more elaborate version for piano or for some combination of instruments in your class.

J. Make a setting of the following text or another text of your choice for three-part chorus. Include in your setting examples of the following:

> Neapolitan triad
> Mode mixture
> Common-chord modulation

Your composition should begin and end in the same key. Be sure to include a harmonic analysis.

> A storm of white petals,
> Buds throwing open baby fists
> Into hands of broad flowers.

—From "The Year," in *Cornhuskers* by Carl Sandburg

Chapter 22

AUGMENTED SIXTH CHORDS

EXERCISE 22-1

A. For each exercise that follows, provide the key signature, and then notate $\sharp\hat{4}$ to $\hat{5}$ on the top staff and $\hat{6}$ to $\hat{5}$ (or, in major, $\flat\hat{6}$ to $\hat{5}$) on the bottom staff. Finally, show an analysis of the implied chords as in the example.

B. Label each chord, using bass-position symbols where appropriate.

c♯: _____   b: _____   f: _____   E♭: _____   D: _____

d: _____   D♭: _____   a: _____   g: _____   b: _____

C. Notate each chord in close position. Augmented sixth chords should be in their customary bass position (6̂ in the bass in minor, ♭6̂ in major). Include key signatures.

B♭: Fr+6   d: N6   b♭: Ger+6   A♭: It+6   B: ii∅6̸5

f♯: It+6   A: Ger+6   c: Fr+6   G: vii°7/vi   e: Ger+6

D. Label the chords in each example that follows. Also, discuss the details of the resolution of each augmented sixth chord. Do $\sharp\hat{4}$ and ($\flat$) $\hat{6}$ follow their expected resolutions to $\hat{5}$? How are parallel 5ths avoided in the Ger^{+6} resolution(s)?

1. This waltz begins with a chord that, until it resolves, sounds like a V^7 in what key? Are there any other references to that key in the excerpt?

Schumann, Waltz op. 124, no. 4

2. As you might guess, an enharmonically spelled $^{+6}$ chord occurs in this excerpt. Label the chords.

Koffman, "Swinging Shepherd Blues"

3. This excerpt begins in C major and modulates. Find two 9–8 suspensions.

Haydn, String Quartet op. 74, no. 3, II

4. Measures 2–5 of this excerpt are in d minor, although the key of VI (B♭) is strongly tonicized in mm. 2–3 (the second chord in m. 2 should be analyzed as a secondary function of VI). Common-chord modulations to two other keys occur in mm. 5–11.

Schumann, "Sehnsucht," op. 51, no. 1

Ich blick' _____ in mein Herz _____ und ich blick' _____ in die Welt, bis vom

schwim - mem - den Au - ge die Thrä - ne mir fällt; wohl

leuch - tet die Fer - ne mit gol - de-nem Licht, doch

hält mich der Nord, _____ ich er - rei - che sie nicht. O die

Schran - ken so eng, _____ und die Welt _____ so weit,

5. This excerpt begins and ends in g minor, but it contains modulations to two other keys (or tonicizations of two other chords). How do those keys relate to the "parent" tonality of g minor?

Schumann, "Die beiden Grenadiere," op. 49, no. 1

Kind   zu Haus,   die   oh - ne mich   ver - der - ben."   "Was schert mich   Weib,

6. This very chromatic excerpt from an early Mozart string quartet contains an augmented sixth chord that resolves quite irregularly. Before you begin to label the chords, review the use of the subdominant chord in minor on pp. 57–58 and on p. 245.

 Mozart, String Quartet K. 168, II (piano arrangement)

c:

7. The slow tempo of this theme allows some measures to contain several chords. In the first measure, for example, each bass note is harmonized by a new chord, with the exception of the B2. Discuss the various uses of the pitch class G♯/A♭ in this excerpt.

 Beethoven, String Trio op. 9, no. 3, II

8. This excerpt will give you practice with both alto and tenor clefs. Label all chords and NCTs. The final cadence at first combines a V^7 with elements of the tonic triad.

 Schubert, String Trio D. 471

$$\frac{(V^7)}{I - - - - - -}$$

9. This excerpt modulates to the dominant, passing through another key on the way. The first chord in m. 8 is spelled enharmonically (imagine a G♮ instead of the F𝄪). Be sure to analyze a chord on beat 2 of m. 8.

Schumann, Tragödie, op. 136, no. 3

Ent - flich' mit mir und sei mein Weib und ruh' an

mei - nem Her - zen aus! In wei - ter Fer - ne sei mein

Herz dir Va - ter - land und Va - ter - haus!

Name_____ Class_____ Date_____

E. Supply the missing voices for each of the following fragments. All are four-part textures.

g: ii⌀$^4_3$ It^{+6} V   F: IV^6 Ger^{+6} I$^6_4$ V   c: vii$^{o4}_2$ Fr^{+6} i$^6_4$ V

D: vi   IV^6 Fr^{+6} V^7 I   b: ii⌀$^6_5$ (i$^6_4$)   Ger^{+6} (i$^6_4$)   V$^4_2$ i^6

F. Complete these harmonizations, adding one or two inner voices, as specified.

e: i   Ger^{+6} i   E♭:   I   It^{+6} I

a: i   Fr^{+6} i   B♭:   I   It^{+6} I

G. Analyze the harmonies specified by this figured bass, and then make an arrangement for SATB chorus.

H. Analyze the harmonies implied by this soprano/bass framework, being sure to include an It^{+6}. Then, fill in the inner voices, following good voice-leading procedures. There are no NCTs in the bass and soprano lines.

I. Given next are mm. 1–2 of a four-measure phrase. Continue the passage to make a period (parallel or contrasting) that ends with a PAC in the key of the dominant. Include an augmented sixth chord.

Chapter 23

ENHARMONIC SPELLINGS AND ENHARMONIC MODULATIONS

EXERCISE 23-1

A. Analyze the given chord. Then, show any possible enharmonic reinterpretation(s) of that chord, keeping the same key signature. The enharmonic reinterpretation should involve a new key, not just an enharmonically equivalent key (such as g♯ and a♭). Number 1 is supplied as an example.

F: $\underline{V^7/IV}$ = A: $\underline{Ger^{+6}}$ g: _____ = _____   D: _____ = _____

B♭: _____ = _____ = _____ = _____   F♯: _____ = _____

B. Each of the following short passages contains an enharmonic modulation. Analyze each passage after playing it slowly at the piano and listening for the point of modulation. Do not try to analyze these passages without hearing them.

2

3

C. Analyze the progressions implied by these soprano and bass lines and fill in the inner voices. Analyze enharmonic common chords where indicated.

Use two different chords on the last beat of m. 2 and the first beat of m. 3 in Exercise 1.

1

b: i   V

2

C: I

D. Compose short passages similar to those in Part B. The given chord is to serve as the common chord in an enharmonic modulation. (Hint: As you sketch out your progression, notate the given chord first. Then, find satisfactory ways to lead into and away from that chord.)

1. G to B. Common chord: V^7/IV in G.

2. b to B♭. Common chord: vii^{o7}/iv in b.

3. B♭ to E. Common chord: vii^{o6}_5 in B♭.

4. E to F. Common chord: Ger^{+6} in E.

E. Analysis. Be sure to play as much as you can of each excerpt.

   1. This passage modulates from f♯ minor to A♭ major by way of E major. The bass notes are found above the "*Ped.*" markings—the other notes in the bass clef are arpeggiations into inner voices. Label all the chords, including common chords for both modulations.

Chopin, Nocturne op. 27, no. 1

2. This excerpt begins in G minor. Label all the chords.

Beethoven, Piano Sonata op. 13, I

3. This excerpt is from the end of the exposition and the beginning of the development of a movement in sonata form (review pp. 338–348 in Chapter 20). The final cadence of the last B theme is shown in the first few measures of the excerpt (in E♭ major). The music then leads to a modulation to C minor in the first ending and to A minor in the second ending. Notice that the sonority first heard in m. 76 is used again twice, each time in a different way. (Bonus question: What *other* sonority in these measures is treated enharmonically?)

Brahms, String Quartet op. 51, no. 1, I

4. The next excerpt is quite challenging. Label both chords and NCTs. You might find it helpful to label the chords with lead-sheet symbols before assigning roman numerals.

Haydn, String Quartet op. 76, no. 6, II

5. This dance modulates from D♭ to A and back again. Although both modulations involve enharmonicism, only one of them is a true enharmonic modulation—the other uses enharmonic spellings for convenience.

    a. Label all the chords, including two common-chord modulations.

    b. Label the enharmonic modulation.

    c. Discuss the form of this piece.

    Schubert, Originaltänze, op. 9 (D. 365), no. 14

F. Use mm. 31–34 of Part E, number 4, as the first phrase of an eight-measure parallel period. The second phrase should include an enharmonic modulation to a foreign key.

G. Compose the beginning of a song with piano accompaniment, using a text of your choice. Include two enharmonic modulations, one of them using a Ger^{+6} chord, the other a diminished seventh chord. Include analysis.

Chapter 24

FURTHER ELEMENTS OF THE HARMONIC VOCABULARY

EXERCISE 24-1

A. In each fragment that follows, analyze the given chord. Then, notate the specified chord
in such a way that it leads smoothly into the given chord with acceptable voice leading.
Some of the problems use a five-part texture for simpler voice leading.

D: IV^M9 _____   E♭:   (ct°7) _____   b: V^7subs._____   A: V^+7 _____
                                                          6th

F♯:   (ct°7) _____   B♭: V^+6/IV _____   E: ii∅4/3 _____   g: V^♭9 _____

B. Compose four short passages for piano, each one making use of a different progression from Part A. The half-note durations do not need to be retained, but use the same voice leading.

C. Analysis. Throughout this section, highlight (using arrows or whatever is convenient)
   any occurrences of the chords discussed in this chapter.

1. Label chords and NCTs.

 Schumann, *Humoresque*, op. 20

2. This excerpt features one of the chords discussed in the chapter. The last chord in m. 8
   should be analyzed as a secondary function. What is the form of the excerpt?

 Chopin, Nocturne op. 32, no. 2

3. a. Analyze this excerpt in f minor throughout. One of the chords is best analyzed as a chord with an added 6th.

b. Put parentheses around NCTs, and be prepared to discuss them.

c. Diagram the phrase structure, and label the form. Assume four-measure phrases.

 Chopin, Mazurka op. 63, no. 2

4. This excerpt (the title translates literally as "On Quiet Forest Path"), composed in the 1880s, is a fine example of the late Romantic style. It contains a modulation to a foreign key, but the common chord, which we have located for you, is not often used in this way.

  Strauss, "Auf stillem Waldespfad," op. 9, no. 1

Thanks to Richard Bass for this example.

5. Harmonic sequences occupy most of this excerpt.

   a. Find the two sequences and bracket each occurrence of the sequential patterns.

   b. If it is possible to do so, label the chords in the sequences with roman numerals, perhaps in terms of shifting tonalities.

   c. Discuss briefly the large-scale harmonic/melodic function of each sequence. In other words, just what does each sequence accomplish harmonically and melodically? (An excerpt from the beginning of this song appears on p. 151 of this workbook.)

Schumann, "Die Löwenbraut," op. 31, no. 1

Die un - se - li - ge wagt's sich der Thü-re zu nah'n, da fällt er ver wan - delt die Her-rin an, die schö-ne Ge - stalt, ein gräss-li-cher Raub, liegt blu-tig zer - ris-sen ent - stellt in dem Staub.

Und wie er ver-gos - sen das theu - re Blut,

6. This familiar excerpt is easier to listen to than it is to analyze. The transpositions do not make the analysis any easier—clarinets in A and horns in F—nor do the four clefs in use. Do your best with the score (after all, conductors face this sort of problem every day), and then check your work with the piano reduction that follows the excerpt.

Tchaikovsky, Symphony no. 6, op. 74, I

7. The chord in m. 4 should be analyzed in two ways: the way in which we expect it to resolve when we first hear it and the way it actually functions.

Schubert, *Schwanengesang*, "Kriegers Ahnung"

8. This excerpt ends with an enharmonic modulation leading to a cadence that implies the key of e, although it is not confirmed by the following phrase.

 Schubert, String Quintet, op. 163, I (piano reduction)

Chapter 25

TONAL HARMONY IN THE LATE NINETEENTH CENTURY

EXERCISE 25-1

A. Total voice-leading distance. You are given several pairs of chords. For each pair, do the following:

1. Label each chord using lead-sheet and bass position symbols (e.g.: F$\sharp^{\sharp o 4}_{\sharp 3}$).

2. Indicate the distance between roots by interval (e.g.: m3). Use the appropriate enharmonic interval.

3. Calculate the total voice-leading distance between each pair of chords in half steps.

Chord: D$\sharp$m^6 B$\flat^6_4$ ——   ——   ——   ——   ——

Root int.:   +3   ——   ——   ——   ——   ——

Total dist.:   2   ——   ——   ——   ——   ——

Chord: ——   ——   ——   ——   ——   ——

Root int.: ——   ——   ——   ——   ——

Total dist.: ——   ——   ——   ——   ——

Which chord pair(s) above are in a chromatic mediant relationship? _____

Which chord pair(s) above are in a doubly chromatic mediant relationship? _____

253

B. Examine the first 25 measures of the opening of *Tannhäuser*, given below, and do the following:

1. The opening eight measures show rather traditional harmonic functions. Analyze these measures, using roman numerals (do all work on the music).

2. The following eight measures, which may also be analyzed with roman numerals, show less-traditional harmonic movement. Cite at least three examples of such nontraditional features [show measure number(s)].

   a. _____

   b. _____

   c. _____

3. In the score, analyze the sequence that begins in m. 16, beat 3 and continues through m. 21, beat 1 using lead-sheet and bass-position symbols. Circle those chords that are most strongly tonicized. What is the relationship between these circled chords?

   _____

Wagner, *Tannhäuser*, Prelude to act I (piano reduction)

C. Analyze the following chromatic sequences, then continue each as indicated.

1

2

Select one of the preceding sequence patterns to serve as the basis for a piano composition. You might want to create a melody over the background of block chords or perhaps modify the texture of the harmonies themselves. Nonessential or embellishing chords may be inserted within the sequence for the purpose of color.

D. Continue the following sequences as indicated. Then, select one to serve as the harmonic basis for a piano or vocal composition in the style of one of the post-Romantic composers studied. Strive for contrapuntal interest and smooth voice leading.

1

2

3

E. Examine the following excerpt.

♫ **1.** The opening key is designated as E major. What is interesting about the structure of the scale that forms the basis for mm. 2–3? _____

_____

_____

2. Provide roman numeral analysis for m. 2. _____

In what way does the music in mm. 10–11 suggest a more traditional treatment of tonality?

_____

_____

3. Describe the modulatory procedure that takes place in mm. 12 to 13. _____

_____

_____

4. Name the key introduced in m. 14. _____

What is its relationship to the opening key? _____

5. Name two other keys hinted at between mm. 1 and 14. _____

and _____ These keys represent what relationship to each other and

to the opening key? _____

Wolf, "Die ihr schwebet um diese Palmen"

F.   Examine the following excerpt.

   ♪   **1.** Is there a clear tonal center in the opening five measures? If so, what is it, and how
        is it defined? _____

        _____

   2. Name the three different sonorities in mm. 6–8 using lead-sheet symbols. _____,
        _____, and _____

        On the staff below, rewrite these three chords so that they progress by shortest total voice-leading distance.
        List each distance by number of half steps in the blanks provided. The first chord is already shown.

        Total voice-leading dist.: _____   _____

        As you can see, these chords can be connected quite smoothly. Why do you think Wolf
        might not have chosen the smoothest possible connection between the three chords?

        _____

   3. What roman numerals are used in mm. 9–12 to prepare the cadence in D major?

m. 9	m. 10	m. 11	m. 12

        What is the relationship between the chords on the downbeats of mm. 9–10?

        _____

G. Given the following pairs of chords, notate the inversion of the second chord that connects most smoothly with the first chord as given. Indicate the total voice-leading distance in the space provided. Ignore traditional resolutions (leading tones, sevenths, etc.). There may be more than one right answer.

1 DM$^4_2$ F#^{7}
dist.: _____

2 E♭m$^4_3$ C^7
_____

3 G$^{o6}_5$ Dm^7
_____

4 Fr^{+6} D♭^{7}
_____

5 Em$^4_2$ G^{o7}
_____

6 Fm^7 A♭m^7
_____

7 A$^{ø6}_5$ B^7
_____

8 G^7 B♭M^7
_____

H. The following excerpt is taken from the final movement of the Piano Trio, op. 3 by Ernest Chausson (mm. 159–174).

1. Analyze this excerpt using lead-sheet and bass position symbols. Write your answers in the score.

2. Describe the different ways in which chromatic mediant relationships organize this passage.

_____

_____

_____

3. What is the prevailing key for most of this passage? In the absence of the dominant of this key and of other traditional progression types, how does Chausson establish this key?

_____

_____

_____

Chausson, Piano Trio, op. 3, IV

I. **1.** In the following *Siegfried* excerpt, analyze one essential harmony for each of the
first 11 measures of the excerpt.

    m. 1   m. 2   m. 3   m. 4   m. 5   m. 6   m. 7   m. 8   m. 9   m. 10 m. 11

2. Name at least three keys (including the first one) that are established throughout the course
of this excerpt. Show the measure numbers.

_____   _____   _____

3. Show two instances in which modulation is effected by deceptive resolution, either of
chords or of single pitches. Describe the process that takes place.

_____

_____

_____

Wagner, *Siegfried* (act III, scene 3)

J. **1.** The following excerpt begins and ends in E major. What is unusual about the manner in which the key is established in mm. 10–13? _____

_____

_____

2. Label the harmonies found in mm. 14–22. Use lead-sheet symbols for your analysis.

3. What five-chord succession within mm. 14–22 represents an "omnibus" fragment?

_____

4. In what way is the approach to the closing E major harmony unusual? _____

_____

_____

5. By what means does Fauré make it convincing, nonetheless? _____

_____

_____

_____

Fauré, "Chanson d'Amour," op. 27, no. 1 (mm. 10–22)

Part VI
An Introduction to Twentieth-Century Music

Chapter 26

MATERIALS AND TECHNIQUES

EXERCISE 26-1

A. Add the appropriate accidentals to create the modal scale indicated.

C-Mixolydian   C-Dorian

C-Phrygian   C-Lydian

C-Aeolian   C-Locrian

B. Add the appropriate accidentals to create the modal scale indicated.

D-Mixolydian

B-Dorian

F-Phrygian

G-Aeolian

E-Lydian

G-Locrian

C. Answer the following questions about the diatonic modes.

1. The three modes that are essentially *major* in quality are the _____, _____, and _____ modes.

2. The three modes that are essentially *minor* in quality are the _____, _____, and _____ modes.

3. All the modes contain a perfect 5th from $\hat{1}$ up to $\hat{5}$, except the _____ mode.

4. The two modes that contain a leading tone are the _____ and _____ modes.

5. The two modes that contain a minor second from $\hat{1}$ up to $\hat{2}$ are the _____ and _____ modes.

6. The $\hat{1}-\hat{4}$ tetrachord in the Mixolydian mode matches that of the _____ mode.

7. Likewise, the opening tetrachords of the Aeolian and _____ modes are the same.

8. The four modes that contain a major 6th from $\hat{1}$ up to $\hat{6}$ are the _____, _____, _____, and _____ modes.

9. The three modes that contain a minor 6th from $\hat{1}$ up to $\hat{6}$ are the _____, _____, and _____ modes.

10. Name the interval from $\hat{1}$ up to $\hat{4}$ in the Ionian mode. _____

11. Name the interval from $\hat{1}$ up to $\hat{4}$ in the Lydian mode. _____

12. Name the interval from $\hat{4}$ up to $\hat{7}$ in the Ionian mode. _____

13. Name the interval from $\hat{4}$ up to $\hat{7}$ in the Mixolydian mode. _____

D. Using a key signature (rather than appropriate accidentals), notate the following modal scales in the clef indicated.

A♭-Ionian

D-Locrian

D-Phrygian

A-Phrygian

F#-Dorian

F#-Aeolian

E. Notate the following pentatonic and synthetic scales starting on the pitch indicated. Be sure to include the octave-related pitch.

Major pentatonic

Minor pentatonic

Hirajoshi pentatonic

Lydian-Mixolydian

Lydian-Mixolydian

Phrygian-Dorian

F. Notate the following symmetrical scales starting on the pitch indicated. Be sure to include the octave-related pitch.

G. Add the appropriate accidentals (or delete the appropriate notes) to create the scale indicated. You may choose a starting pitch of B or B♭.

H. Identify the scale used in the following passages.

1 ♩ = ca. 84

_____

2 Allegretto

_____

3 Moderato

_____

4 ♩ = ca. 108

5 ♩. = ca. 72

6 Moderately

Name_____ Class_____ Date_____

I. Analysis. The following examples represent three versions of the principal tune from Debussy's "Fêtes." For each, identify the scale being used.

Debussy's "Fêtes," from *Nocturnes* (piano reduction)

scale: _____

scale: _____

mm. 29–32

scale: _____

J. Composition.

Using the major pentatonic scale B♭–C–D–F–G–B♭ as a basis, compose five brief melodies, each of which in turn establishes the indicated tone as a tone center. (Hint: D is tough. Why?)

1

2

3

4

5

Create a melody based on the octatonic scale that emphasizes major and minor 3rds.
Carefully use rhythmic interest to create an exciting melody.

6

Create a melody based on the hexatonic scale that emphasizes major and minor triads.
Carefully use rhythmic interest to create an exciting melody.

7

Create a two-voice composition based on a whole-tone or octatonic scale. You might want to create a symmetrical relationship between the two voices or perhaps treat them imitatively. If your composition is for piano, experiment with the wide range of the keyboard.

8

EXERCISE 26-2

A. Describe the structure of the following chords by providing the correct symbol: Use the symbol "Q" for quartal/quintal chords, "S" for secundal chords, and lead-sheet symbols for tertian sonorities and polychords.

B. Identify the following sonorities as a quartal/quintal chord (Q), split-third chord (ST), whole-tone chord (WT), or tone cluster (TC).

C. Describe the types of vertical sonorities found in the following examples as tertian, polychordal, quartal, quintal, or added-note.

3

4

D. Complete the following passages using chromatic planing. That is, use the given initial
sonority to create a passage where all voices move in the same direction by the same
interval.

E. Complete the following passages using diatonic planing. That is, use the given initial sonority to create a passage where all voices move in the same direction by the same diatonic interval within the key signature indicated.

F. Complete the following passages, using the triad type indicated for each hand. Continue the scoring suggested by the first polychord, using the given outer parts consistently as either roots, 3rds, or 5ths of the sonority.

1 R.H. major, L.H. major

2 R.H. minor, L.H. minor

3 R.H. major, L.H. minor

4 R.H. major, L.H. minor

G. Analysis. Listen to the following example and answer the following questions.

1. What technique is used to create form in this piano composition?

_____

2. Notate the scale that forms the basis of the opening *four* measures:

_____

Does the piece have a tone center? _____ If so, what is it? _____

If you do not perceive one, why? _____

3. What are the distinguishing characteristics of the opening two measures? _____

_____

_____

4. In what ways is the character of the opening maintained throughout the piece?

_____

_____

5. What is the derivation of the thematic gesture found in m. 3 of the right-hand part?

_____

Locate three other instances in which that intervallic pattern appears (other than in the bass line).

a. _____

b. _____

c. _____

Payne, *Arch*

H. Composition. With the help of your instructor, execute one or more of the following composition projects. Take great care in the preparation of your score and prepare a performance for class.

1. Compose a short piece that features extended tertian harmony—for example, ninth, eleventh, and thirteenth chords.

2. Compose a short piece that features quartal harmony.

3. Compose a short piece that blends tertian, added-tone, and quartal harmonies.

4. Compose a short piece that features whole-tone chords.

5. Compose a short piece that features polychords.

6. Compose a short piece that features a variety of sonorities derived from a major pentatonic scale.

7. Compose a short piece that features chromatic-mediant relationships or polychords derived from the octatonic scale.

8. Compose a short piece that features traditional triads and seventh chords derived from the octatonic scale.

9. Compose a short piece based on diatonic planing, chromatic planing, or mixed planing.

10. Compose a short piece that illustrates the principles of pandiatonicism.

EXERCISE 26-3

A. Which of the following rhythmic procedures—added value, asymmetric meter, displaced accent, metric modulation, mixed meter, or nonretrogradable rhythm—are illustrated by the following examples?

1

_____

2

_____

3

_____

4

_____

5

_____

6

_____

B. Messiaen's rhythmic procedures.

   1. Which of the following rhythms are nonretrogradable?

   2. Consider the rhythmic figure:

   Identify the added value in the following rhythms by marking it with a "+" symbol.

C. Answer the following questions about the terms and concepts mentioned in the Rhythm and Meter section of Chapter 26.

1. _____ is an interaction between rhythm and meter that implies a 3:2 ratio.

2. Music that lacks an aurally perceivable meter is called _____ music.

3. The simultaneous presentation of two or more strikingly contrasted rhythmic streams is called _____.

4. _____ rhythm refers to the listener's perception that unequal groupings of subdivisions are being added together.

5. A _____ bar line can be used to indicate irregular subdivisions of the bar.

6. Traditional meters, such as $\frac{4}{4}, \frac{2}{4}, \frac{3}{4}, \frac{6}{8}$, etc., are often referred to as _____ meters because they are based on regular recurring pulses that are subdivided into groups of two or three.

7. A musical pattern that is repeated many times in succession is called an

_____.

8. The modern term for a rhythmic technique associated with Medieval motets and masses, an

_____, typically consists of a repeated rhythmic figure called the _____

in combination with a repeated pitch sequence of a different length called the

_____.

9. An immediate change in tempo created by equating a particular note value to another note

value, a proportional note value, usually located in the next bar, is called a _____

_____.

10. The Fibonacci sequence is an infinite sequence of numbers that can be written, for example,

1, 1, 2, 3, _____ , _____ , _____ , _____ , _____ , _____ , 89, etc.

11. Each member of the Fibonacci sequence is the sum of the previous

_____ numbers.

12. The consecutive ratios implied by the Fibonacci sequence—for example, 3:2, 5:3, 8:5,

13:8, etc.—approach the _____ _____ (ca. 1.618:1),

a proportion found throughout nature that has also been associated with proportional balance in art and architecture.

13. The simultaneous use of two or more strikingly contrasted tempos is called

_____.

14. A canon in which the individual voices are presented at different tempos is called a

_____ _____.

D. Analysis. Comment on the rhythmic and metric devices employed in the following excerpts.

Stravinsky, "Danse de la foire," from Petrouchka (piano reduction)

E. Composition. With the help of your instructor, execute one or more of the following composition projects. Take great care in the preparation of your score, and prepare a performance for class.

1. Create a polyrhythmic composition for two percussionists. Use any two like nonpitched percussion instruments (claves, cowbells, hand-claps, etc.).

2. Create a composition for any two instruments that features a passage based on polymeter.

3. Create a composition that utilizes two or more of the following rhythmic devices: added value, asymmetric meter, displaced accent, metric modulation, or mixed meter.

Chapter 27

POST-TONAL THEORY

EXERCISE 27-1

A. Mod 12 and Pitch Class. Reduce the following integers to an integer mod 12 (0–11 inclusive). Use the pc clockface diagram to aid in your calculations.

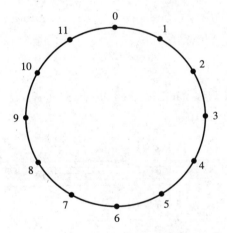

1. 13 _____

2. 15 _____

3. 20 _____

4. 16 _____

5. 23 _____

6. 11 _____

7. 24 _____

8. −5 _____

9. −7 _____

10. −15 _____

B. Transposition (T_n). Transpose the following pc sets given in integer notation [C = 0].

1. T_1 (1,2,3) = _____

2. T_3 (3,6,9) = _____

3. T_6 (7,5,3) = _____

4. T_5 (11,6,1) = _____

5. T_0 (2,9,7) = _____

6. T_8 (2,6,10) = _____

7. T_2 (7,5,3,1) = _____

8. T_9 (3,6,9,0) = _____

9. T_4 (8,0,1,3) = _____

10. T_7 (7,1,6,0) = _____

C. Inversion (T_nI). Invert the following pc sets given in integer notation [C = 0]. Use the two-step procedure shown in the following example.*

	Operation	Set After PC Inversion	Answer
Example	$T_{10}I\,(8,6,5) =$	$T_{10}\,(4,6,7) =$	(2,4,5)
1.	$T_6I\,(1,2,4) =$	$T_6(\_\_\_,\_\_\_,\_\_\_) =$	(___,___,___)
2.	$T_9I\,(7,8,9) =$	$T_9(\_\_\_,\_\_\_,\_\_\_) =$	(___,___,___)
3.	$T_{11}I\,(11,8,7) =$	$T_{11}(\_\_\_,\_\_\_,\_\_\_) =$	(___,___,___)
4.	$T_1I\,(11,8,7) =$	$T_1(\_\_\_,\_\_\_,\_\_\_) =$	(___,___,___)
5.	$T_5I\,(10,9,0,11)$	$T_5(\_\_\_,\_\_\_,\_\_\_,\_\_\_) =$	(___,___,___,___)
6.	$T_0I\,(4,6,5,9) =$	$T_0(\_\_\_,\_\_\_,\_\_\_,\_\_\_) =$	(___,___,___,___)
7.	$T_7I\,(1,0,7,6) =$	$T_7(\_\_\_,\_\_\_,\_\_\_,\_\_\_) =$	(___,___,___,___)
8.	$T_4I\,(2,6,8,4) =$	$T_4(\_\_\_,\_\_\_,\_\_\_,\_\_\_) =$	(___,___,___,___)

*Note that the T_nI operation may also be performed using a one-step procedure. The procedure involves subtracting each member of the set in turn from the index n of T_nI, for instance, in the preceding example:

	Operation	Set After PC Inversion	Answer
	$T_{10}I\,(8,6,5) =$	(10-8,10-6,10-5) =	(2,4,5)

D. Interval Class. Provide the interval class names of the following intervals by using the numbers 0 through 6.

E. Interval Vector. Label each interval in the given pc set using interval classes. Use this
    information to identify the set's interval vector.

1

Interval vector: __ __ __ __ __ __

2

Interval vector: __ __ __ __ __ __

3

Interval vector: __ __ __ __ __ __

4

Interval vector: __ __ __ __ __ __

5

Interval vector: __ __ __ __ __ __

F. Notate the given pc set using staff notation in the space provided. Then, provide the set's normal form (using letter names) and prime form (using pc numbers).

1 PC Set: (A,E,E♭)

STAFF NOTATION WORKSPACE

Normal form: [__,__,__]

Prime form: (__ __ __)

2 PC Set: (D,A,F♯)

Normal form: [__,__,__]

Prime form: (__ __ __)

3 PC Set: (C♯,G♯,D♯)

Normal form: [__,__,__]

Prime form: (__ __ __)

4 PC Set: (D,E,A,G)

Normal form: [__,__,__,__]

Prime form: (__ __ __ __)

5 PC Set: (B♭,A,C,B)

Normal form: [__,__,__,__]

Prime form: (__ __ __ __)

6 PC Set: (G,F,E♭,D)

Normal form: [__,__,__,__]

Prime form: (__ __ __ __)

G. For each of the following sonorities (trichords and tetrachords), determine the normal
    form, prime form, Forte name, and interval vector.

Normal form: [__,__,__]   [__,__,__]   [__,__,__]   [__,__,__,__]

Set class (Forte name/Prime form):

   3-__ (__ __ __)   3-__ (__ __ __)   3-__ (__ __ __)   4-__ (__ __ __ __)

Interval vector: __ __ __ __ __ __   __ __ __ __ __ __   __ __ __ __ __ __   __ __ __ __ __ __

Normal form: [__,__,__,__]   [__,__,__,__]   [__,__,__,__]   [__,__,__,__]

Set class (Forte name/Prime form):

   4-__ (__ __ __ __)   4-__ (__ __ __ __)   4-__ (__ __ __ __)   4-__ (__ __ __ __)

Interval vector: __ __ __ __ __ __   __ __ __ __ __ __   __ __ __ __ __ __   __ __ __ __ __ __

H. Analysis. *From Ritual to Romance* for solo piano by Reginald Bain, which follows, opens with an atonal passage. Try to play the example and then answer the following questions:

1. Determine the normal form of the initial four-note melodic gesture (C,C♯,G,F♯). To what set class does this pc set belong?

    Normal form: [__, __, __, __] Belongs to set class: 4-__ (__ __ __ __)

2. Find two other melodic instances of this set class in the passage. Circle these occurrences on the score, and mark them with the appropriate Forte name.

3. The three-note melodic cell (G,F♯,B♭) plays an important role in the passage. Determine this set's normal form. To what set class does it belong?

    Normal form: [__, __, __] Belongs to set class: 3-__ (__ __ __)

4. Find four instances of this set class in m. 6. Circle them on the score, and mark them with the appropriate Forte name.

5. Determine the normal form of the chord (B,E,B♭), which occurs in the right hand, m. 2. To what set class does it belong?

    Normal form: [__, __, __] Belongs to set class: 3-__ (__ __ __)

6. Find another instance of this set class in the right hand. Circle it on the score, and mark it with the appropriate Forte name.

7. To what interval class does the left-hand gesture in m. 2 belong?

    ic____

    Is this interval class prominently featured in the set classes you identified above?

    Yes/No (circle one)

8. A new set class begins to play an important role in m. 5. Two occurrences may be found in the right-hand melody, mm. 5–6. What set class is it?

    Set class: 3-__ (__ __ __)

    Circle both occurrences on the score and mark them with the appropriate Forte name.

Bain, *From Ritual to Romance*

I. Composition. Compose a piece according to one of the following specifications, and prepare a performance for class.

1. Create a melody that begins with a statement of set class 3-1 (012) and goes on to emphasize the following interval classes: ic2 (e.g., M2 or m7), ic1 (e.g., m2 or M7), and ic5 (e.g., P4 or P5).

2. Create a composition for piano that is based on two harmonic cells and two melodic cells. For example, you might choose set classes 3-9 (027) and 3-7 (025) for your harmonic cells and ic1 and ic2 for your melodic cells.

EXERCISE 27-2

A. The series given below is from Berg's *Lyric Suite*. Given the P₅ form of the series, notate the I₅ form on the staff provided, then complete the 12 × 12 matrix. Label the series forms using the blanks provided.

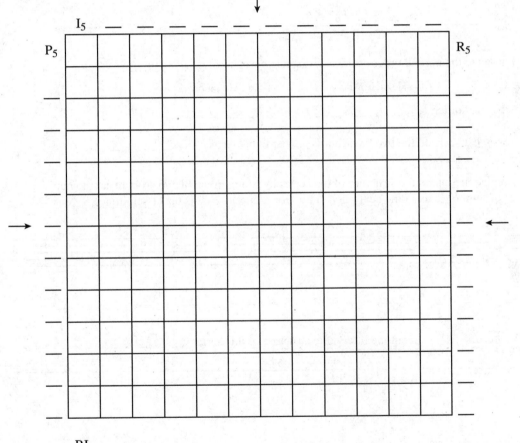

B. Answer the following questions about the structure of the series from Berg's *Lyric Suite*.

1. In the following trichordal segmentation of the series, identify the set class to which each discrete trichord belongs by providing its Forte name and prime form.

3-__ (__ __ __)   3-__ (__ __ __)   3-__ (__ __ __)   3-__ (__ __ __)

2. In the following tetrachordal segmentation of the series, identify the set class to which each discrete tetrachord belongs by providing its Forte name and prime form.

4-__ (__ __ __ __)   4-__ (__ __ __ __)   4-__ (__ __ __ __)

3. Determine the normal order of the two discrete hexachords.

                1st Hexachord   2nd Hexachord

Normal order: [__, __, __, __, __, __]   [__, __, __, __, __, __]

From what scale do the two hexachords appear to be derived? The _____ scale.

4. Examine the intervallic structure of the series by filling in the blanks to indicate the number of semitones up to the next pitch class. For example, F–E is up 11 semitones.

<u>11</u>   __   __   __   __   __   __   __   __   __   __

What is interesting about the intervallic structure of this series? _____

_____

C. Series Forms. Given the P_2 form of the series from Schoenberg's *Fourth String Quartet*, op. 37:

P_2

Notate the following series forms. The first note has been provided for you.

1 P_7

2 R_2

3 R_7

4 I_2

5 I_7

6 RI_8

D. Analysis

1. "Full Moon" (from *Twelve 12-Tone Pieces for Children*) by Otto Joachim is based on a 12-tone series. It employs a single series form: P_7. First, identify the series, and notate it (using the treble clef) on the staff provided. (Hint: The series is presented for the first time in mm. 1–3. The order of the pitch classes in m. 3 is E♭–B♭–G♭–D♭.)

P_7

Order
numbers: 1   2   3   4   5   6   7   8   9   10   11   12

Now indicate occurrences of the series in mm. 1–24 by marking series form symbols (remember, the piece employs only P_7) and order numbers (1–12) on the score.

Full moon

Otto Joachim

Name_____ Class_____ Date_____

In some ways, "Full Moon" sounds almost impressionistic. What compositional devices has the composer employed to create this effect?

_____

_____

_____

2. "The Moon Rises" by Ernst Krenek is based on the following 12-tone series:

Order
numbers: 1   2   3   4   5   6   7   8   9   10   11   12

Like Joachim's "Full Moon," it employs a single series form (P₃). Trace the presentation of the series throughout the course of the piece by marking series form symbols and order numbers (1–12) on the score.

Krenek, "The Moon Rises," No. 4 from *Twelve Short Piano Pieces*, op. 83

3. *Twelve Short Piano Pieces*, Op. 83, by Ernst Krenek, is based on the following 12-tones series. In preparation for the work that follows, notate the I_5 and R_5 forms of the series on the staves provided:

In examining the music, you will note that the first measure of the right hand opens with the first three notes of I_5, whereas the left hand features the first two notes of R_5. The third note of this latter series form is D♭. It is accommodated by the right hand because the third note of I_5 is also a D♭. Following this, the roles of the series forms are reversed, with the left hand picking up I_5 while the right hand continues with R_5. Because of the frequency of this type of exchange where two or more series forms are involved, it is helpful to enclose I_5 row numbers in rectangles and R_5 numbers in ovals.

Krenek, "Glass Figures," from *Twelve Short Piano Pieces,* op. 83, no. 8

4. Composition. Using the series for "The Moon Rises," shown next, compose a two-voice composition, the upper voice of which is based on a transposed series form while the lower voice makes use of a retrograde series form. You might want to try using instruments other than piano, such as violin and cello or two flutes.

EXERCISE 27-3

A. Answer the following questions about integral serialism.

1. The term *total serialization* refers to the process whereby parameters other than pitch, such as _____, _____, and _____, are decided on by means of a predetermined series.

2. Two composers associated with the origins of total serialization are _____ and _____.

3. The French composer _____ composed *Structures Ia* (1952), a work in which the pitch series was adapted from Messiaen's *Mode de valeurs et d'intensités* (1949).

4. The American composer _____ was evidently the first to explore the serialization of elements other than pitch in *Three Compositions for Piano* (1947).

B. Analysis.

1. With the help of your instructor, find a work that illustrates the principles of integral serialism. Analyze and write a summary of the work.

C. Composition.

1. Compose a short piece featuring elements of total serialization. Prepare a performance for class.

Chapter 28

NEW DIRECTIONS

EXERCISE 28-1

A. Answer the following questions about the terms and concepts mentioned in Chapter 28.

1. John Cage composed works for _____ _____ that involved the placement of various objects and/or materials on the strings of the piano at precisely specified locations.

2. The system of tuning in which the intervals are represented using whole-number ratios is called _____ _____.

3. The interval that divides the octave into 24 equal parts is called the _____ _____.

4. The scores for George Crumb's *Makrokosmos* and Krzysztof Penderecki's *Threnody to the Victims of Hiroshima* are examples of _____ _____, a notational style that uses nontraditional symbols to represent musical information.

5. _____ _____ is a notational style that indicates approximate durations through the spacing of events and timings.

6. Compositions created out of sound masses distinguished not by pitch but by timbre, rhythm, density, register, and so forth are called _____ - _____ _____.

7. György Ligeti used the term _____ to describe the canonic relationships between the voices in the complex, clusterlike surfaces of his early orchestral works.

8. The extended vocal technique associated with Arnold Schoenberg's *Pierrot lunaire* is called _____, a cross between singing and dramatic declamation.

9. Gunther Schuller led a movement called _____ - _____, which blended elements of jazz and serious contemporary music.

10. _____ or _____ refers to music in which elements of a composition have intentionally been left undetermined by the composer.

11. In *Music of Changes* (1951) for solo piano, John Cage used _____ _____ derived from the *I Ching*, the ancient Chinese *Book of Changes*, to determine the work's pitches, durations, dynamics, and so forth.

12. John Cage helped to initiate the _____ _____ tradition with works such as *Imaginary Landscape No. 4* (1951) for 12 radios and *4'33"* (1952).

13. The term _____ refers to a style that seems to have evolved out of the music of John Cage and Morton Feldman and is characterized by a return to tonal elements and diatonicism, as well as the use of restricted pitch materials, static harmony, and rhythmic elements inspired by Eastern music.

14. The concept of _____ is a compositional process associated with the music of Steve Reich in which two identical copies of a musical pattern are allowed to drift out of phase with one another. The rich surface texture that results is essentially the product of unforeseen _____ _____ that are created by the constantly shifting relationship between the parts.

15. Examples of early electronic instruments include the _____, _____ _____, and _____.

16. Music that exists primarily in the medium of magnetic tape is called _____ _____.

17. Pierre Schaeffer's approach to electronic music in which he worked directly with recorded sounds, organizing them into musical structures without the use of traditional notation, is called _____ _____.

18. The _____ _____ _____ spans ca. 20 Hz to 20,000 Hz.

19. An _____ _____ gives musical shape to an oscillator's static tone by imparting an attack, decay, sustain, and release phase to the tone's overall loudness profile.

20. The introduction of _____ _____ _____ in the 1960s, marketed under trade names of Moog, Buchla, and ARP, offered a wide palette of new electronic sounds.

21. Released in 1983, the Yamaha DX-7 was one of the first commercially successful _____. It was based on an _____ _____ technique discovered by John Chowning at Stanford in the late 1960s.

22. A software application that stores sequences of MIDI data is called a _____.

23. Iannis Xenakis is perhaps best known for his _____ _____, in which the musical parameters such as pitch, intensity, and duration are determined by the laws of probability theory.

24. Tod Machover coined the term _____ to refer to his use of computers to augment musical expression and creativity.

25. The underlying tonal basis of many of Paul Lansky's computer-generated compositions has caused some to describe these complex works as a form of _____, a term used to refer to music that seems to have its roots in the minimalist traditions of the 1960s and 1970s.

B. Analysis. With the help of your instructor and appropriate secondary sources:

1. Find a work that illustrates the use of expanded textural, timbral, or tuning resources. Analyze and write a summary of the piece.

2. Find a work that illustrates the principles of indeterminacy. Analyze and write a summary of the piece.

3. Find a work that illustrates the principles of minimalism. Analyze and write a summary of the piece.

4. Find a work that illustrates the principles of the new vocalism. Analyze and write a summary of the piece.

5. Find a work that is an example of *musique concrète*. Analyze and write a summary of the piece.

6. Find a work that is, strictly speaking, an example of electronic music. Analyze and write a summary of the piece.

7. Find a work that uses electronic means of any sort to reinterpret a work by a well-known Baroque, Classical, or Romantic composer. Analyze and write a summary of the piece.

8. Find a work that combines live performer and recorded music (tape, CD, etc.) or real-time interaction with a computer. Analyze and write a summary of the piece.

C. Composition. With the help of your instructor, execute one or more of the following composition projects. Take great care in the preparation of your score and performance directions. Prepare a performance for class.

1. Compose a short piece featuring aleatoric or indeterminate elements.

2. Compose a short piece featuring special effects for your instrument or voice.

3. Compose a short piece with a nontraditional score that features both graphic and proportional notation.

4. Compose a short piece that is based on an alternative tuning system (quarter tones, just intonation, etc.).

5. Compose a short piece that features tone clusters and that is based on the principles of sound-mass composition.

6. Compose a short piece that blends elements of jazz and serious contemporary music.

7. Compose a short minimalist piece based on the concept of phasing. Use a one-measure melodic gesture as the basis for the work.

8. Compose a short electronic composition using music software that is freely available over the Internet.

Name_____ Class_____ Date_____

Tonal Harmony

Name_____ Class_____ Date_____

Tonal Harmony

Audio Recordings to Accompany Workbook

THE PERFORMERS

Jana Holzmeier, Jennifer Murray, *soprano*
Julia Armstrong, *mezzo-soprano*
Tim Campbell, David L. Jones, David Stevens, Stephen Bathory-Peeler, *tenor*
Eric Swartzentruber, *bass*
Joel Quade, David Small, Richard Womack, *baritone*
Elizabeth Whitten, Chris Devine, *flute*
Mary Ellen Miller, *clarinet*
David Pinkard, *bassoon*
Michael Misner, James Wester, *horn*
Jennifer Bourianoff, Marian Mentel, Colleen McCullough, Chris Devine, *violin*
Greg Snedeker, *cello*
Kyle Sigrest, Reuben Allred, Nadine Shank, *piano*
David Mead, Alejandro Hernandez-Valdez, *piano and harpsichord*
Roger Graybill, Lenore Alford, *organ*
Myra Spector, Tina Marsh, Madalyn Palmer, *jazz vocals*
David Renter, *jazz saxophone*
Jeff Hellmer, Anthony Belfiglio, Miro Sprague, *jazz piano*
Kris Afflerbaugh, *jazz bass*

The Barton Strings
Beth Blackerby, *violin*
Jennifer Bourianoff, *violin and viola*
Martha Carapetyan, Bruce Williams, *viola*
Carolyn Blubaugh-Hagler, *violoncello*

Tosca String Quartet
Leigh Mahoney, *1st violin*
Tracy Seeger Beth Blackerby, *2nd violin*
Ames Asbell, *viola*
Sara Nelson, *cello*

Chamber Choir—David Mead, *conductor*
Judith Kanana, Carol Hopkins, *soprano*
Brooke Lehr, Kellie McCurdy, *contralto*
Oliver Worthington, *tenor*
Te Oti Rakena, Steven Olivares, *bass*

Orchestra—David Mead, Alejandro Hernandez Valdez, *conductors*
Elizabeth Whitten, Michelle Clover Neal, *flute*
Pamela Whitcomb, Lana Neal, *oboe*
Marisa Bannworth Wester, Shannon Thompson, *clarinet*
David Pinkard, Rhonda Collison, *bassoon*
James Wester, Michael Misner, Richard Wheatley, Kellie Babcock, *horn*
Thomas Caswell, Stephen Miles, *trumpet*
Sean Scot Reed, David Garcia, David Hendricksen, *trombone*
Richard Short, *timpani*
Marian Mentel, *concertmaster*; Tera Shimizu, *principal violin II*
Jennifer Fedie, Wei He, Daniel McAtee, Sean Milligan, Hye-Sung Oh, Sue-Jean Park, Linda Piatt, Thomas Sender, Marvin Suson, Alicija Usarek, *violin*
Joseph Tan, Mark Sattler, Jason Elinoff, *viola*
Paul Rhodes, Kirsten Eggen, Sara Nelson, Victorial Wolff, *violoncello*
John Rosenkrans, Robert Jenkins, *contrabass*

Mark Ellis, *announcer*
David Mead, Alejandro Hernandez-Valdez, Anthony Suter, Andrew Murphy, *producers*
Andrew Murphy, Frank Simon, Greg Snedeker, *engineers*
J. Burke Hunn, Michael Czysz, *assistant engineers*